Seven Ages of Nursing

Mark Radcliffe MA, RMN

Acknowledgements
I'd like to thank Captain Kirk, Bobby Crush, Mister Ed, Princess Anne, Scooby Doo and all of the Banana Splits, especially Snorkey. However, there really is no point because I don't know them and they don't know me. Furthermore, Princess Anne, Bobby Crush and maybe Mister Ed have done nothing to improve the quality of my life so I wish I hadn't even mentioned them. Still, what's done is done.

On the other hand, the hundreds of nurses I have worked and played with have been more than helpful. They have bought me drinks and lent me footwear.

Particular thanks go to friends at NT, especially Deborah, Val, Martin and Brian who between them came up with more stories than that big building in Towering Inferno.

Extra special super-duper thanks to Kate, David, Gail, Ursula, Tracy and Una.

The whole thing is dedicated to my mum because she likes a laugh and is the best nurse I've ever known.

Produced for Nursing Times Books by Monkey Puzzle Media Ltd, Gissing's Farm, Fressingfield, Suffolk IP21 5SH, UK

First published 1998 by Nursing Times Books, Emap Healthcare Ltd, part of Emap Business Communications, Greater London House, London NW1 7EJ

Printed and bound in Great Britain by Ashford Colour Press, Gosport, Hampshire

British Library Cataloguing in Publication Data
A catalogue record for this book is available from the British Library.

ISBN: 1 902499 24 7

Disclaimer
Names, places, characters and incidents are either products of the author's imagination or, where true, names and details have been changed.

Contents

Introduction

◆ ◆ ◆ ◆ ◆ ◆ ◆

Nursing is the new rock and roll. Nursing is a sexy, living on the edge, leather-trouser wearing, guitar solo kind of thing. It throws TV sets out of hotel windows (metaphorically of course – we wouldn't want to hurt anyone). It curls its lip at crass and lifeless TV presenters and estate agents. In an era where not wearing sensible shoes is about as radical as people get, nursing flies in the face of convention and says: 'No actually I'm not going to become a mechanical engineer or something in computers or go into landscape gardening or try to get a job on a soap opera. I'm going to nurse, for nursing is the new rock and roll.'

The activity of nursing is challenging and useful, and that is so un-1990s. The obvious way to be useful if you were young a couple of years ago was to become an environmental warrior but you had to change your name to Spunky or Biff the Flower Saver. Which may be fine now but in 20 years time when you are working in a garden centre or as an accountant you really won't want to be saddled with the name Biff the Flower Saver. How many successful accountancy firms do you know who practice in the name of Ford, Grimshaw and Biff the Flower Saver?

However the fact that nursing is the new rock and roll is not wholly good news. Rock and roll is by its nature a thing of fashion. Only a few years ago poetry was the new rock and roll. This was characterised by broody young men in long coats. It was of course never going to catch on. Try all you like but until someone comes up with a word that rhymes with 'orange' the poets are stuffed. That's why, for example, the poet laureate Ted Hughes only ever writes about stoats and badgers and stuff. Loads of things rhyme with badger:

I love to watch the badger.
I wonder if I could catch her.

(Tell Ted he can have that one if he wants)

After poetry came gardening. Alan Titchmarsh was the new Elton John. Thinner, obviously, but gardening was where it was at.

Herbaceous borders were the new drum and bass until, and this came as a particular blow to those of us who like to dabble under a hedge, everyone noticed that gardening was terribly dull.

A few other activities tried to be the next rock and roll. People who work for the major municipal companies had a go at turning the sale of electrical goods into the new rock and roll but they rather missed the point. Rock and roll itself has had a go at being the new rock and roll but everyone just got confused, and in one of the saddest attempts at being the new rock and roll ever seen, geography teachers clubbed together and drove an old Rolls Royce into a swimming pool. Nobody was impressed, even though the pool was empty, geography teachers are more Millican and Nesbit than T Rex.

If you think about it logically (which is, perhaps, unwise, given the possibility that you are going to read the rest of this book), nursing is just about the only genuinely stylish, significant and generally cool job left, not including vet, international jewel thief, overseas aid worker or someone who drives those really big bulldozers. Apart from those, there is nothing that is genuinely adventurous left to us.

It may be that the government's new recruitment drive will shortly use the 'Nursing is the New Rock and Roll' slogan in a series of TV adverts. I rather like the idea of a string of Rock'n'Rollers like David Bowie, Chrissie Hynde, Damon Albarn, Nana Mouskouri, Cerys of Catatonia, some Nolans and George Michael, looking earnestly into a camera saying 'On the whole I wish I'd become a nurse,' before picking up their bags and walking down the street. In the background will be a montage of songs with the word 'angel' in the title (this will be ironic, as the look on the faces of all the pop stars will demonstrate for those of you who, like America, don't get irony). Then the advert will fade to real-life nurses doing some bits of nursing to a backdrop of 'Heroes' and the occasional shot of Bowie looking bemused, then 'Heroes' gets taken off the record player by an irritated nurse who puts on any chart-topping foot-tapping hit she likes to show the world that nurses are just normal in a 'special' kind of way. Cue deep sigh, and a telephone number that impressionable people watching too much television can phone to find out more about not being a pop star.

Maybe not, then.

It may be the case that a myth prevails as to who it is who actually nurses. The myth has it that the typical nurse lives in Hertfordshire, she may be married, to a man who has a side parting and two suits, neither of which he chose himself. They are a quiet couple who are active in the local community. She may be single, in which case she lives in Plymouth and collects cats and Tupperware. She is waiting for Crimplene to make a comeback and enjoys many things including needlepoint and Perry Como. She listens to the pronouncements of her leaders with a respectful interest. She may be a he, in which case he is gay, which is fine so long as he doesn't try to force his sexuality down anyone's throat, so to speak. He may be a he and not gay in which case, if he is a general nurse he is perhaps destined for a managerial position sooner than if he is a she, which is for the best because he'd make the wards look untidy and we can't really expect him to do proper nursing for too long because of genetics and stuff.

The mythical nurse has little better to do with her time off than think about her time on. She is obedient (in a modern way), restrained and austere. She is a professional and proud of it. The organisations that speak to nursing speak directly to her. The authors who write, write mainly for her, and the academics who have all the time in the world to set about designing this modern profession design it around her. However, recent evidence suggests that there are only two mythical nurses left in the country. The other half a million or so are irritatingly different.

Some of them are a bit like her, in that they think often about their 'profession', others in that they mourn the loss of Crimplene. Some however don't care much for pronouncements on professionalisation or PREP or anything else really. They know how to do what they do rather well, and they enjoy doing it most of the time, although frankly sometimes the beaurocracy and stress hacks them right off. They are more likely to be interested in what their colleagues think about the day than in what their leaders plan for the future, they are more interested in the weekend than in the latest piece of research on wound care that is blowing up a storm in America. Some of these nurses probably nurse better than any chief nurse this country has ever had, they probably know implicitly as much about how to save a life as any Professor in Europe, and they are all probably better dancers than anyone who works for the RCN. In fact some of them are only ever touched by the agenda that is set by academics, policy makers and regulatory bodies when their plans become law. Basically there are lots of nurses and they deal with what they do in lots of different ways; and as long as they do their jobs well then it is impossible to suggest that any one way is better than any other.

The thing that unites nurses is the nature of our experience. We have all seen things, felt things and managed things that other people haven't. Other people may be curious about them (even if often we appear not to be) and that is why it is now the law that there is a television programme about nursing on every night. But it isn't quite the same. Nurses nurse, and after they have nursed each day they go dancing or for a drink or to kick their cat, or travel to Plymouth to kick a mythical nurse, or they go home to make Airfix models or have interesting sex or they hitchhike to Peru or scuba dive or party or sleep. Sometimes they hang out with other nurses and talk about their day or the job or anything except their day or the job. And, when they hang out and drink and mock and laugh and play they are still nurses.

This is a book for nurses who hang out and drink and play and laugh. Its voice is the voice of the pub or the coffee room or the bus ride home. It is the nursing voice I am most familiar with from 12 years of nursing. I am sorely tempted to lay claim to a subtext that seeks to deconstruct the didactic austerity that pervades nursing. To claim some grand purpose of political and cultural revolution, in the hope that if enough people mock or ignore nonsense, then nonsense will shut up or go off to bother another profession like policemen or electrical goods salespeople. I would like to claim that this book is a simple but honest attempt to quietly ripple the waters of professionalisation – which I have to say strikes me as an idea borrowed from the 1970s and if they were going to borrow an idea from the 1970s I wish they'd taken the lava lamp. However that would all be self-justifying crap. Basically I'm just having a laugh.

I would like to say however that it is not my intention to be rude. If I have in any way offended anyone, their beliefs about nursing, their investment in making the activity a better-regulated, better-researched place to be then I can only say that you really should not take yourselves so seriously.

Finally, about the ponies. I mean every word I say.

The Student

◆ ◆ ◆ ◆ ◆ ◆ ◆

Hello, welcome, glad you could come. Now before you got here everyone spent about 20 years arguing about what kind of training we could offer you. We wanted something comprehensive, in keeping with the modern image of a modern profession. Something that included a sound clinical base, the personal development opportunities that would enable you to cope with the experiences and stresses that are so integral to the job. And the intellectual and academic skills to enable you to theorise effectively about nursing as a science whilst augmenting your critical skills, thus allowing you to make appropriate and informed clinical decisions. We also needed you to develop the human ability to comfort, reassure and inform your patients. To allow you to advocate on behalf of your patients, to communicate with them and with colleagues with equal ease and efficiency. We needed you to acquire a vast range of technical skills and the wisdom to judge which of them is useful. Most importantly perhaps, we needed to offer you the emotional capacity to live in the stories of the people you work with. To hold hands with the dying, to listen, quietly, and to know when or if or how to respond. We needed to offer you a training that would arm you, equip you to meet the avalanche of need you will face, and we want you to feel enabled, in 10 years' time to feel privileged, useful, wise and, most importantly, unbroken.

However we couldn't think of anything so you got Project 2000.

Please don't be put off. Despite everything you may hear to the contrary, nurse training has always been more endurance test than well-planned educational opportunity. The fact that we all romanticise about our nurse training, despite how hellish it may have been, is because the experience was and always will be so powerful it's hard to let go of it. Sometimes maybe we feel threatened that that experience will be lost or undervalued and so we get protective. At other times we find ourselves believing in the way we practice and the foundations of that good practice, and imagine they are under threat. At yet other times we are afraid of what you might not know, forgetting all the things that we did not know. However on other occasions, and let's be blunt about this, we are going to come across one or two bad apples that could spoil an otherwise good barrel. We should no more be put off by them than we should by the frailties of an education system that sometimes lets you down.

As a student you are going to have to endure many pointless things. There will be times on the wards when bored staff, anxious to prove to you that they have a sense of humour, will send you next door for 'a long stand' (geddit?). You will probably know that this is called a practical joke. However you should know that you have three choices. You can go next door for a while, stand about a bit then come back and let them have their fun. Which is generous of you but means that a few days later they may send you off for a left-handed syringe, the little pranksters. Or you can say cordially, 'I'm sorry but I do not believe in the long stand myth, please don't waste my time I'm trying to nurse here,' which no matter how polite you are will gain you the reputation of being a smug know-it-all with no sense of humour. Or you could say, 'Sod off with the long stand gag you sad git,' which, whilst justified, may put a strain on your student-preceptor relationship.

Whilst on the ward, if you are planning to be a general nurse there will be much talk about hats and stuff. This needn't be taken too seriously. It will essentially be just a precursor to the many conversations you will hear that will start with the words, 'In my day...' as in, 'In my day we did proper nursing...', 'In my day we didn't have buses and we had to walk up to 20 miles a day just to do a shift and we wore our hats,' and 'In my day we didn't have fancy colleges, with your books and well-stocked fizzy drink dispensing machines, you lot don't know you're born.' Still, in fairness, you will meet some people who nurse as well as Sinatra sang. For all the talk that surrounds your chosen profession, occasionally you see some work, or maybe do some work that makes you feel as though the planet you find yourself on finally fits. So don't worry about the long stand nonsense.

In the class rooms and lecture halls, of course, things can be different. The chances are some of the tutors are human, friendly, intelligent and supportive. But some of them are tossers. Imagine, if you are a woman, arriving at a party to find it filled with 15-year-old boys all desperate to impress you. They will not listen to anything you say, they will not ask you anything, and after drivelling on about nothing for about an hour they may try to persuade you to admire them by doing unsightly sit-ups on the carpet. If you don't clap or snog them they will call you names and maybe pull your hair. Well some nurse tutors are a bit like that. They will often drivel on for hours but probably won't do the sit ups. These are insecure people. Ignore them, they have no friends, they have come to education late and consider it something to be conquered rather than embraced. You can always tell a good teacher: s/he makes ideas understandable and accessible no matter how complex they are, because they want to share them in the hope that you will use them. No single idea in nursing is difficult to convey. If it sounds difficult it can only be because the teacher is a fool or he wants to impress you with his sit-ups. It is important that you do not take him seriously. Invent a stupid name for him; 'smudger' was popular in the 1950s, 'faceache' in the 1960s, but since then we have pretty much stuck with a 'dickhead' theme, with a few variations according to any specific quality you may want to highlight.

One of the things you are likely to find as a student is that nursing is an activity steeped in a rich history of local and national myth. For example, my friend Victoria Blame tells of her first day on a medical ward, near the end of her training in a large London teaching hospital. She was shown round the fire exits, the intensive care beds, the kettle and finally – the sluice room. At this point her nurse guide began to look a little embarrassed and for the first time began to falter in instructions. Victoria, who is the Keeper of the Truth, quickly picked up on her new colleague's sudden discomfort and said:

'Shona, we have never met and to you I am a stranger but we are now colleagues and I hope one day friends. Now I sense that you are uncomfortable about something here but I know not what. Now Shona, I notice things and you may know that I am the Keeper of the Truth. I want you to tell me exactly what it is that is making you uncomfortable.'

'Why are you calling me Shona?'

'Is that not your name, Shona?'

'No my name is Kevin.'

'I had no way of knowing.'

'Well, it's on my badge, and I am wearing trousers, and I introduced myself to you less than five minutes ago and I am married to your sister.'

'Oh yes, it's coming back now' said Victoria 'but I'm right in thinking there is something wrong am I not?'

'It's uncanny Victoria, you are right. I wish you'd noticed the whole boy-called-Kevin thing, but there you go. Your talents obviously lie elsewhere. Somewhere other than noticing the gender of the brother in law you work with …'

'Yes yes get on with it' said the Keeper of the Truth.

'Well, it's about the sluice. It makes funny, sometimes embarrassing noises.'

'What sort of funny noises?'

'It's hard to describe …'

Victoria, having heard many a sluice, began to do impressions of sluices she has known, whirring and chugging away until she went quite pink. At this point the sister came in. Victoria was embarrassed, but needn't have been; the sister merely said:

'My, what an impressive array of sluice impressions. I can hardly wait for the Christmas party. What we would give for a sluice that made sounds like that. Can you do any other impressions? A horse maybe? Or Tommy Cooper?'

Victoria confirmed that she could indeed do a very fine impression of a horse and started cantering around the sluice room with Kevin on her back, whinnying and clippety-clopping away like, well, a horse. Everyone was impressed but the sister quite rightly put a stop to the revelry and sent the nurses back to work.

Later that evening Victoria, alone this time and a little tired, had to use the sluice for the first time. What was that sound? It was strange, eerie almost. And then she realised. The sluice whirred to the tune of 'Chattanooga Choo Choo' with barbershop quartet harmonies.

It appears that a member of a barbershop quartet had died on that ward almost 50 years ago and his colleagues, essentially a trio waiting to happen, had tried but failed to get to his bedside to pay their last respects. His dying wish was to hear, for one last time, 'Chattanooga Choo Choo' but he never did. And now every time the sluice is used that song reverberates around the ward.

This is just one example of nursing folklore. There are a million others out there, some absurd some spooky, most made up on tea breaks, but all an integral part of nursing. Take the story of Cathy Thyme.

A student nurse in the 1960s, Cathy was the sort of nurse who prompted the enviable comment, 'Oh she's got a lovely way with the patients, they all love her.' Some said Cathy was born to nurse. However she was dyslexic. In those days dyslexia attracted little sympathy or understanding and consequently many occasions arose that made her feel stupid. She was not stupid but she became insecure. The day before her finals an incident occurred on the drug round where Cathy was struggling with a long word and called for assistance. Under the circumstances this was a skilful and safe decision and because of it no drug error was made; however a cruel junior doctor who looked a bit like Alec Baldwin and behaved like Terry-Thomas teased her mercilessly, calling her stupid and illiterate. She was neither but in keeping with her background, her gender, and the way of some nurses in those days, she felt stupid and illiterate.

The next day she attended her final exam. She was well equipped, she had pens and pencils, she even had a protractor. Of course nobody knows what a protractor is for but everyone takes them into exams in case they need them. More importantly she knew everything a student about to qualify needed to know. With the words of the junior doctor ringing in her ears she answered every question required, handed in her paper and tidied away her pencils and mathematical aids knowing that she had passed. Then she went back to her room in the nurses' home and hanged herself.

Legend has it however that this was not the end of Cathy's nursing career. A friend of mine who worked in the same hospital tells that on three separate occasions in the last 30 years when a young student nurse of much promise has struggled for reasons outside of her control, perhaps in the face of the stresses of the job or more commonly the thoughtless bullying of an arrogant medic, the ghost of Cathy Thyme appears. She rests a reassuring hand on the shoulder of the struggling nurse and, after waiting for an appropriate moment in the routine of the ward, she kicks the shit out of the doctor.

Look out.

In my day, training was based on the apprenticeship model. This essentially consisted of being thrown at wards and staff as early as possible and told to learn how to nurse by copying other nurses. It was a painful process. For apprenticeship models to work you pretty much need the Yoda method, I think. That is, you the student nurse need to be paired with some green-eared muppet with all the answers, who will teach you to nurse like a space warrior. However, in reality you tended to get given whoever was not on duty when the charge nurse asked the question, 'So who wants the next student then?' As you changed wards every three months your learning experience was down to chance. In practice it was a bit of a disaster.

However, in principle at least and if you were lucky and quite determined, there was a bit of an education in there that could be squeezed out. The simple priority of being with patients and learning from them was clear. However we were forced to confront our own ignorance a dozen times a day in what was often a hostile environment. One of the big pluses was the fact that we trained in small, easy-to-store groups of about 15. Usually at least three people dropped out so about a dozen of us spent three years together and we got to know each other quite well. I trained in one of the old, now long defunct 'bins'. We started with six weeks in what was then called 'school' and then we were thrown at the elderly mentally ill back-wards and left there for three months. Apparently this was done because the powers that be felt that if you were going to be driven out by the hopelessness in the walls of those old spiteful asylums, it would save money and time to get you out early.

We were encouraged to use our group as a major form of support, which we did. We learnt to nurse in much the same way as you, I suspect, by sitting around getting drunk, howling at the moon and comparing horror stories. We swore we would be better than what we saw, and never indulge ourselves with pointless confrontation. Our training in that environment was an exercise in developing strategies for change. We took comfort from each other's outrage and anger, and plotted ways of making tiny alterations. My first was to try to make sure that demented old ladies were never fed whilst they were defecating. A small thing perhaps but it seemed a good place to make a stand. Our stands were like signatures, proving to ourselves we had been in this timeless place and had left a mark of sorts. Such was our romance.

Frankly it was all terribly emotional, a bit like a Bette Davis film. Perhaps we were pathetic. All clean and righteous. Surrounded by staff who had been there longer than the patients. But it is, I suspect, a history shared by some of the staff who irritate you now. I think the reality is that the problem you are forced to endure is a clash of cultures. Yours is different from ours.

And let's not imagine that in the world of general nursing things were wonderful either. Victoria Blame trained in the olden days when dance music was called 'disco' and Spandau Ballet happened.

She reports that on her first ward, after a mere six weeks, she was repeatedly sent by the senior staff nurse to whom she was assigned to 'prepare the trolley for a chest drip' or to 'resite and set the saline'. Thus Victoria was forced to spend all day saying she did not know how to do that and being treated as a fool. She tells how the wards then were not really focused on patients but instead on routines. She herself was once strongly reprimanded by a sister for wheeling a trolley to a bedside, in preparation for doing a dressing, but committing the heinous crime of taping the disposal bag to the trolley in such a way as to appear unsymmetrical. Her punishment? She had to do 50 press ups and swear never to tape anything to a trolley without using a protractor again. It was important that the students learnt in those days that the wheels of a trolley when stationary had to all face the same direction.

She tells also of one of her first ward rounds, when the God known as consultant arrived on the ward and began to pronounce on the sick. Irritatingly one of the patients was having a shave at the time of the great man's arrival, so the consultant marched to the semi-bearded patient and, without saying a word, unplugged the electric razor before returning to take centre stage. No nurse did a thing, although later another student, to his eternal credit, complained at the handover that this was no way to treat the patients and that surely we, the nurses, should be stopping this sort of pomposity. He was threatened with dismissal. This was in 1987. Not 1895.

It's worth remembering that the same nurses who tell you that everything used to be better, and that patient care always came first, often trained under these circumstances. In a climate of fear, the activity of nursing was a series of tasks; patients were occasionally irritating distractions from the routine of the ward. In the same way perhaps that human beings are the bane of an architect's life, patients were sometimes the fly in the otherwise aseptic ointment of ward life. My friend Rita Blood cried every night for a month when she started nursing. Not because of the suffering she saw but because of the nonsense she had to endure to become a nurse. I don't imagine that for one second, when you as a student are taking nonsense in whatever form you may find it, you can take comfort from the fact that nonsense is some kind of hereditary arrangement in nursing, but it may do no harm to de-romanticise the whole 'in my day we did proper nursing' rubbish. A lot of people did, but a lot more polished stuff, deferred to unthinking medics and made the students' lives a misery.

When I ask Rita how she coped she says, as many people do, that she came across one or two people who inspired her. Romance again? Probably not. Rita tells of working on an elderly unit with terribly institutionalised, unthinking staff with long and poorly formed habits. Apparently a newly arrived sister, who came to nursing late and with an energy and enthusiasm that put her younger colleagues to shame, set out to challenge some of the less savoury elements of care. For example, was it really necessary to prepare the patients for bed at four o'clock in the afternoon and make sure they had all retired, after toileting, by five? One suspects not, unless they all had a paper round to get up for. And why was it that none of the patients ever left the ward? This woman started arranging trips to the shops, to the seaside; she changed the ward routine as best she could.

A few years later Rita met the nice lady again doing agency work with the district nurses. She was planning to take early retirement, she had lost weight and faith. Her staff had stopped talking to her, she had found a dead mouse in her desk drawer, three days in a row. Mouse flu suggested her staff? She left. Things went back to normal.

Things weren't better in those days. In fact, things were crap. What was better perhaps was that the lines between doing your job well and doing it badly were clearer. The possibility of doing a good thing in the face of the bad was greater. The struggle was simple, if sometimes seemingly impossible. And like people remember the ugliness of wars with a sense of misplaced glee, then some nurses recall their struggles because they were life affirming.

Part of the rationale for P2000 was to protect students from that rubbish and to sterilise and perhaps dignify the process of learning to nurse. I would applaud that but, and I realise I should apologise for this, I hope you have your battles too. I hope you see things that make the blood course through your veins and you change them, slightly, fret about them healthily, because that is the role of a student nurse whether it's written into the curriculum or not.

Nursing now exists in a post-modern age and is not afraid to prove it. A lot of nonsense is imagined about what post-modernism means. Which is of course a trick; it doesn't actually mean anything. It is loosely just a label to mark the end of thinking about things in the way that we have always tended to think about things. Primarily it imagines that absolute philosophical truths no longer exist. It presupposes that history has finished and that God is dead and most importantly – and this is the bit I like best – all cultural activity must be equal. Primarily, perhaps, because the systems of value and meaning that are attached by habit or prejudice or taste are rendered empty. So Mozart is no more significant or worthy than that Shake and Vac advert. So why am I boring you with a crass bastardisation of modern thought? (like I can remember any of this stuff). Well obviously it's an overlong build-up to a stupid story.

As a student nurse you are entering a confusing world. Because, as I said earlier, you are going to be gently teased and have crass practical jokes done near and to you, you may come to doubt many things you hear regardless of how intelligent you are. My friend Rita has been nursing for 13 years. She has run units, worked independently in the voluntary sector and in primary care. She has a degree in law, which she took part-time because she wanted to be stimulated by something other than nursing. She has a Master's degree in organisation psychology. I don't know why she did that; I think she wanted to organise stuff. She currently works as a health visitor. However on her first ward whilst training she received a seemingly ridiculous circular sent to all the new nurses and to this day, and despite herself, she cannot quite decide if it was somebody's idea of a joke or if it was serious. Such is the strange world of nursing.

The circular said: 'All female nurses are instructed to wear tights. Stockings are not permitted in this hospital. This is because of the infection control implications of pubic fallout.'

It is quite probable that they were serious. Indeed most general nurses of around my age say they experienced the same thing. But how was it to be checked? And by whom?

I imagine that a large part of your experience, which separates you from all the nurses who trained before you, is the relationship you have with the new universities. I don't envy you this. Quite simply in the past, pre-Thatcher certainly, when people went to university (or polytechnic as they were often called in olden days) it was to read interesting books and have sex with unlikely people. Of course you picked up a degree but the process became more important than the goal and the goal tended to be, for a lot of people at least, vague and unfocused. Real world things like nursing were too important for the universities and the universities were too self-absorbed and sober and formal to concern themselves with such realities. Obviously there were 'vocational' courses available but they were in things like engineering and business studies and nobody spoke to the people who did things like that.

Now of course you are between a rock and a hard place. The credibility gap punishes you and there is little you can do about it except find a way to spit in the eye of the snobs and curse the insecure fools who play into the hands of tradition by trying constantly to 'prove' that they and nursing are academically worthy. You are in a poverty trap and may find it hard to enjoy the social setting of university because often nursing is stuck in a small off-campus college away from other students. You may find you share bits of courses with social scientists, which must be vile, and the biological scientists, which must be dull. And when they get long school-like holidays and take their washing home to parents you get sent to do something like work in all sorts of hospital and health care settings where you may not find you are always greeted with open arms.

Perhaps one of the most disgusting and frustrating limits that comes with the 'special status' that accompanies nurse education in the universities is the strange thing known as a bursary.

Yes, it's a little more than a grant but God help you if you get ill or break a limb or some other misfortune. You will have your bursary stopped. You will not get any sick pay, you cannot sign on because you will have to leave your course, you cannot go to the hardship fund because it won't cover illness. You are, and I choose my words carefully here, buggered.

It's all well and good trying to attract people into nursing but as soon as you get here you realise the welfare rights they are afforded are apparently modelled on the system designed by the same bloke who designed the woollen swimsuit. And I don't mean that in a good way. In fact the administration of your student experience does, from the outside, look remarkably similar to a woollen swimsuit, full of holes and difficult to iron. Here we are crying out for new nurses, mourning the lack of new recruits, anxiously trying to attract people in spite of the crises of morale and terrible wages and it would appear that all the training places are full with a massive overflow of applicants and nowhere for them to go. Still, no doubt our greatest nursing minds are on the case and we can expect somebody to round up the usual suspects, form a sub-committee, give them a grant and a nice room with biscuits, and ask them to urgently come up with a solution (more training opportunities perhaps? Sorry I'm guessing) and to have it written up in draft form for the civil service by 2023 at the latest.

Sorry about the state of things, it's one of the problems with social experimentation, because for all the planning and good intentions it's down to you to make it work.

Another significant problem is the fact that you may feel baseless. The university is not quite home, particularly if you are in an isolated college and they may have contracts with about 154 different clinical environments. You are always a visitor, always passing through. Wherever you lay your hat, that's your head, another town another hotel room. You are like Clint Eastwood was in those spaghetti westerns, always moving from town to town, doing good, maybe shooting Eli Wallach. You are the stranger in town. And while we are swimming around in cultural references, do you remember that song called 'I've been to Paradise but I've never been to me'? No reason, just wondered.

The universities get more money per head for you than for any other student. So it's reasonable to expect little presents from the tutors and the administrators, just as a way of them thanking you for your efforts and for your choosing to be a nurse. Everyone benefits from you making the choice you have made: the profession, the universities, the patients, the state, the companies that make nursing accessories. No doubt you will be given a list by someone at some point, outlining all the accessories that you or your parents must buy for you. Whoever gives you the list probably has shares in the company. You will think it odd that you don't get all this stuff for free so think carefully when you look at the list. Do you really need all this stuff?

Uniforms, fob watch, books, belt, several pairs of practical pants, tights, sensible shoes, maybe so. But do you need the special nurse whistle? Or the special nurse moped with 'I'm a nurse' painted on the side? Do you need your own thermometer or stethoscope? I don't think you do. Mental health nurses, do you need even one sociology book? Of course not. And put back that special nurse chocolate cake, it's not an essential tool of your trade. And don't pay for those handouts in lectures or from the library either, how many times are you supposed to have to pay for your education?

Nursing often attracts a more mature student. Some of them can be really really old, like 22. Often even older. This is a good thing but for the mature student it can be an added responsibility. Apart from the fact that you older ones will feel obliged to listen to a whole range of personal issues from fellow students from all kinds of courses, issues including home-sickness, sexual identity, sexual inadequacy, never having had sex, having just had sex and not knowing who is supposed to apologise first, having figured out, post-sex, who has to apologise but not knowing who should pick the pizza. Then there's unrequited love, getting first-time drunks home without them throwing up on you, existential angst (this is compulsory by the way. It is the law that during your university days you have to ask yourself loads of times what the point of everything is and sigh hopelessly because nobody understands what a sensitive soul you are). You will play parent and consequently you may not be given permission to play at the student parties. Well I suggest you play and be damned, if you want to drink crème de menthe from the trouser pocket of the senior lecturer go right ahead. The good thing about being mature is that most things you do that are in fact ridiculous look quite cool to the young. Take the crème de menthe thing for example. Go ahead, sip away, unless said educator is wearing cords obviously because they can feel a bit coarse round the lip I gather, but otherwise sip away, the kids will think it's some kind of rock and roll thing.

It is more than possible of course that you may have grown-up commitments like family and thus any hope of 'living the student experience' is perhaps limited. It is said that being a mature entrant in nursing is something of a two-edged sword. However I can't comment on that because I have no idea what it means. Can you have a one-edged sword? Or a four-edged sword, which one imagines is basically a long square lump of metal with a handle ... Anyway. On the one hand if you are a mature entrant you are likely to have many life skills that you bring to the training. You may have actually had other jobs, you may have been a health care assistant or a civil servant or a swimming instructor or a paper boy. All of these things will equip you for your future in nursing with the possible exception of swimming instructor, although, having said that, if there's a flood you will be the one your colleagues rely on. Have you ever seen the Poseidon Adventure? That bit where a plump Shelley Winters does the underwater swimming? If you are nursing on an overturned cruise ship in the middle of the ocean your pre-nursing life could come into its own.

The down side is you may not be used to the language and convention of modern study. You will of course get used to it, but in the meantime enjoy not knowing. In the research methods class, talk of your commitment to 'evidence-based rashes' and 'random patrol trials'. When they tell you that you are expected to write a long essay before qualifying ask them, 'How long does the end-of-course vivisection have to be?'. When they shout 'dissertation', say 'bless you'.

In the main you may find yourself feeling the strangest things during your training, from rage and despair to compulsion and profound if sometimes unfocused satisfaction. For all the supposed reductionism of nursing and the twee professionalisation, what you are going to be doing for as long as you do it will bring you as close or closer to the nature of things than any other activity. Enjoy, and if all that silly unnecessary essay writing bugs you, don't worry, it has sod all to do with nursing. In the words of the once-lovely David Bowie, obviously before his Tin Machine days: 'If the homework gets you down throw the books on the fire and we'll take the car down town'. Give us a call; I have a car.

THE 'D' GRADE

◆ ◆ ◆ ◆ ◆ ◆ ◆

Congratulations. The first thing you are going to need is a decent meal and some new shoes. You are probably so in debt at this point that you finished your nurse training in flip-flops. Whilst there is little wrong with a flip-flop, in order to get away with wearing them to work you have probably had to camouflage your feet. We all know that it is a massive fashion error to wear socks with flip-flops, so in order to escape the daily foot inspection on your last clinical placement you have probably had to draw a respectable brogue on to your foot with felt tips borrowed from the OT department.

The beauty of this is that you have come to understand more fully the role of the occupational therapy department. All occupational therapists have names that end with vowels. Tanya, Melanie, Dani, Eusebio and Uhuru are perfectly good examples. If you know of an OT whose name does not end with a vowel – Ian, for example, or Skywalker – the chances are they are not real OTs, they may simply be people called Ian who just want to hang out with the girls, or some impressionable space warrior with a dark knight for a dad and a mystical green muppet for a teacher. That can happen a lot; fictional characters from popular culture showing up in strange places. You will get used to it. Think yourself lucky: in my day it was Penelope Pitstop.

It may be the case that your parents, understandably proud of the fact that you have qualified as a nurse and proud that they have raised someone who wants to do something worthwhile with their life rather than be an estate agent, or a motor racing driver, have offered to buy you some new shoes. Your first instinct is to say no. Swallow that instinct unless your parents are very very poor. If they can afford to buy you shoes, take the goddam shoes. If they can afford to buy you a small house, take the goddam house. If they offer to buy you a pony take the pony and free the pony. I don't want to hear that ponies are not supposed to be free, just free the damn pony. Don't strap a stupid saddle to its back and fill its mouth with bridle or whatever, just let the pony go. You don't have to tell your parents, when they want to come and see the little thing get a couple of friends to dress up as a pony. If you are on the mental health branch this will be easy. In any set of 20 mental health nurses there are bound to be at least four with pony disguises.

Anyway, you may think that you are now an independent professional about to enter a desperate job market and you would be kind of right, but you are in for a hell of a surprise when you get paid. Of course it's going to feel like a lot compared to your bursary but that is what is so clever about giving you such a crap bursary. It makes you think that qualifying is the economic light at the end of the tunnel. It isn't; that comes much later when you marry into money or start selling kidneys and running guns in Eastern Europe (don't commit yourself to gun running willy-nilly either, a lot of it happens on a Sunday so you'll be missing out on your unsocial hours).

You see, and you'll find this a lot as time passes, you are getting older now and your tastes and expectations are more sophisticated. A bottle of Thunderbird and an evening of air guitar is not enough any more. You may have a boyfriend, you may have a girlfriend. If you are an RMN the chances are you'll have both and there will be times when you muddle them up. There are obvious advantages to having a boyfriend or a girlfriend. Regular sex is usually a good thing unless of course you are sleeping with someone with a hairy back, which is naturally a bad thing. There are few things in life worse than waking up next to someone who feels like a carpet. You try snuggling up to a hairy back and it's going to itch, you could lose members of your family in there, you yourself may become entangled in the night, and wake up strapped to your lover's back. I hate it when that happens, especially if you are going out that night and you show up at your friend's house entangled and inappropriately dressed. And you can bet she does not have the kind of chairs that facilitate that kind of predicament. What if there's a fire or something and the firemen come and they find you strapped to your lover's back, and she's running away from the flames and you are looking into the abyss known as fire but your hands are not free? 'Blow nurse, with all your puff, blow!' It's all disgustingly Joan of Arc and the last thing you want is Orchestral

Manoeuvres in the Dark writing a song about you.

Still, lovers and partners are useful for other things too: they provide something to talk to your friends about and offer an ear for those end-of-shift rants that are such an integral part of being a nurse. Useful, but expensive: birthdays, Christmas, Valentine's day etc. It all mounts up. There are only so many times you can give your boyfriend a catheter kit. Especially a used one. This is even more difficult if you work in, say, mental health or learning disabilities, because we have so little apparatus to play with.

The Christmas after I qualified I was going out with a similarly newly qualified RMN and neither of us had any money. Of course we agreed, the way lovers do, not to even think about getting each other anything; but at the last moment our resolve broke, we had no money and nothing to steal so we gave each other a nursing intervention. I gave her my look of 'unconditional positive regard'. A handy tool throughout one's life. I raise an eyebrow almost imperceptibly thus demonstrating I notice the behaviour I am being presented with, I almost smile warmly, but not quite, I may stoop forward in order to show a commitment to listening, that kind of thing. I kept this intervention up for the whole morning. My record for unconditional positive regard is four and a half hours and that Christmas I nearly broke it, except my mum came round and said I looked like I had a tummy ache and why didn't I go and sit down.

'I'm giving unconditional positive regard,' I said, in the sulky way grown men use when talking to their mothers.

'Of course you are dear, and we are all terribly impressed, but you look like a cross between Roger Moore and Sid James, so go away.'

I went away. That evening my girlfriend did some active listening on me which was nice, and then we shared an orange. There were people singing carols in the street that night, and it snowed. I think I heard the distant sound of reindeer going home for a well deserved rest; James Stewart was on the television. Strangers called by to say hearty hellos and wish us a merry yuletide. We may have been poor, but it didn't matter because we had stumbled into a cliché and in clichés the poor are always happy.

So the money is crap. There are no easy solutions to this, particularly bearing in mind the inability of unions or organisations to do anything about it. However, in keeping with the creative nature of good nursing, a variety of things have been tried over the years. One of the most splendid schemes involved a young staff nurse I had the pleasure of working with, whom we shall refer to here as Fluffy.

Fluffy once kidnapped RCN headquarters, hiding it under her coat one wet and windy autumn day, and skilfully slipping it through the considerable security arrangements which guard that auspicious if largely pointless organisation. She tricked the clever security team by pointing at the ceiling and saying quite convincingly, 'Ooh look a space monster.' She took the fully staffed RCN headquarters to a small bungalow near Hastings and there she waited. Fluffy watched the news, anticipating quite a kerfuffle. She imagined the headlines: 'Nursing organisation stolen', 'RCN staff kidnapped', and 'Shenanigans in Cavendish Square'. But nothing happened.

Now Fluffy wasn't stupid. She was not going to be tricked into returning the dull and inadequate bureaucracy by anything as transparent as a news black-out and so she waited. And waited. For six years she waited, until finally, when she ran out of supplies, she broke and phoned the authorities. It turned out that nobody had actually noticed that the RCN had been stolen. Fluffy went on to later kidnap large areas of Humberside and a 20-mile stretch of the south-east coast in an effort to force the government to give nurses a fair pay increase. However Fluffy was a nurse, not an urban terrorist. When Humberside and the Isle of Thanet developed a physical relationship she released them and they now form an unsightly and surprising land mass in Wales. Fluffy's efforts failed but yours may not.

I should perhaps stress at this point that I am in no way condoning Fluffy's actions. Please don't kidnap people or buildings. It is neither clever nor grown-up. Appropriating places for personal or professional gain is not dignified. If we are only prepared to be creative there are many many ways in which we can collectively protest against the wages and conditions that nurses are presented with. We could have a national 'wear the wrong hat day' for example. Every nurse in the country, regardless of their location or whether or not they usually wear a hat, could go to work in inappropriate headgear. Yes, you hospital nurses, wear a trilby. Theatre nurses, worried about the infection control implications? Try one of those rubber balaclavas that scuba divers wear. Easy to clean, keeps your ears warm and you don't have to worry about having a bad hair day. Granted we would all look ridiculous and those who insist that nursing must at all times present itself as austere and grown-up may feel their life's work has been destroyed in one hat-wearing day, which is another good reason for doing it. However every time someone says to you, 'Why are you wearing that chef's hat/motor cycle helmet/beret?', you can tell them how much you earn. Lots of media attention, I suspect, and I for one would love to hear Trevor Macdonald say:

'Good evening. All the nurses in the country wore inappropriate hats to work today to protest against continued bad pay. National nurse leaders, when asked why hat wearing had been selected as a form of protest, mainly shrugged. Nurses say that this is just the beginning of a staged protest. Stage two will be carried out by non-nurse sympathisers, who will be asked to march on Downing Street in hats on behalf of the nurses. The National Association for Milliners commented that it wholeheartedly supported the nurses' action.'

No? OK.

One of the things you would have done a lot as a student is swear to yourself repeatedly that when you qualified you would never treat the students the way you were treated. You, unlike the bastards that made your life a misery, would treat the students with respect and courtesy. And you will hold true to this vow, until you get the student we shall call Keith. If you are a mental health nurse Keith will start by asking all the right questions, the things you expect, indeed require of students, stuff like, 'Do you think that drugs are right?' And you think: 'Good place to start, Keith.' And then the next day Keith brings his mum to work. Difficult, you think, especially if you are on an acute admissions ward, but it's good that Keith's mum is showing an interest. And then Keith takes you to one side and says that his mum was feeling a bit low last night and he was wondering if you wouldn't mind having a word. You have a word and discover that Keith's mum isn't so much low as bloody livid. She wants Keith to be a doctor, because he passed his eleven-plus and everything, and nursing is a bit girlie and maybe beneath him because Keith's dad, God rest his soul, was a lawyer. You pass on your condolences to Mrs Keith about Mr Keith's passing, but you are curtly informed that Mr Keith isn't dead; he's living with a masseur called Kurt and now only answers to the name Keithette. Anyway Mrs Keith wants you to keep a special eye on Keith. Make sure he doesn't catch anything like mumps or schizophrenia, and can he come home early when it's dark please. You will do everything possible to avoid having to section Keith's mum but if she does not come in off that ledge before the handover you may have no choice.

If Keith is near the end of his training don't whatever you do ask him what he plans to do when he qualifies. You will be disappointed. It is a proven fact that only 5.7% of newly qualified mental health nurses do any bloody nursing. Most of them want to be psychotherapists. Which is a stupid and unnecessary thing to be and about as useful as an ashtray on a motorbike. I don't know why they want to be psychotherapists; it may be a status thing. I am perfectly aware that when at a party if people ask you what you do and you say, 'I'm a nurse,' one of two things happens. Either they tell you about the last time they were in a hospital and how terrible everything was, but those nurses they do a great job. They say, 'I couldn't do it you know,' and then wander off to the Twiglets. Or they just nod, cough and wander off to the Twiglets.

This is one of the reasons why organisations like the RCN bang on about status so much: they want the word 'nurse' to impress badly dressed, Twiglet-eating inadequates. Waste of time, I say. So Keith imagines that if he responds by saying, 'I'm a psychotherapist,' they will be impressed. Most normal people hear that and think, so, that means you've spent half your salary for the last five years talking to some middle-class berk called Maurice about how your mother's breast milk tasted like sherbet and deep down you suspect she did it on purpose. This represents the tragedy of our age. All the old sins are dead, what we do to others hardly seems to matter. What we feel about ourselves and how we might reframe it for the delectation of others; that is what is supposed to matter. Do you have guilt? Anger? Conflict? These are the modern sins, such is the self-indulgent posturing of the late 20th century. I blame Freud in part. If he could have got a girlfriend none of this would have happened.

If Keith comes to you, the RGN, he will tell you that he has a degree in history and finds nurse training a bit tiresome, but he wanted to work with people. 'By the way,' he may add, 'where are all the people?'. You will tell him that mostly they are the long fleshy things in the beds. He will want to stand near the doctors a lot and will laugh happily when mistaken for a medic. He will buy a stethoscope for absolutely no bloody reason and will ask questions like 'What's his diagnosis nurse?' and 'What care plan?'. Keith won't come to your parties, mostly because you won't invite him, but if he qualifies you can rest assured he will rise through the ranks quickly. Mainly this will happen because he is a boy. Equality in nursing is, as you know, a bit of a myth.

Of course because you are a nurse and because like the rest of us you have experienced things that you perhaps did not immediately understand, you try to contain any resentment or irritation you may harbour. That is until Keith does what he did on Rita Blood's ward several years ago.

Near the end of his second year he was coming to the end of a placement on a surgical ward, a late shift as it happens, when one of the patients arrested. The ward sister, an experienced and calming influence in a crisis, began resuscitation with the help of a staff nurse. She told Keith to go and phone the arrest team.

Keith reappeared a minute or so later and said nothing.

'Did you call the arrest team?' the breathless sister asked without looking up.

'I tried,' said Keith 'but they were engaged. I thought I'd give it a couple of minutes. Shall I get on with something else then?'

Come in planet Keith, this is Earth calling.

You didn't notice Keith when he was in your set did you? Well let me tell you now he was the self-promoting little git who joined all the nursing clubs. The guy who had mapped out a career before he'd so much as given a bed bath. Keith was the one who took the RCN seriously, to the point whereby he was a student advisor before he could take a blood pressure, and who had the UKCC Code of Conduct poster on his bedroom wall next to his pictures of Billy Joel and Prince Andrew. Yes, all students are equal, but not all students are the same. You will get some who manage to remind you of everything good about the job with one intervention. And you will get Keith. The hardest thing you will do, as long as you nurse, is to sustain yourself. You will have little in reserve for the Keiths of this world. Of course there is another possible explanation for your distaste for the many impressive and good students, those who are inspiring and committed. You may be a qualified Keith.

You may find being a D grade is the hardest nursey thing to be. I think I did. On the one hand you know enough to understand the importance of doing things well and properly, on the other you have seen enough and are self aware enough to know that there are things you do not feel confident with. Don't worry, stay curious, play to your strengths and it seems to come together. You get more patient contact than you are likely to get later on, and that is where the confidence comes from.

But also look out for the little lapses that may befall you, often through little fault of your own, and often fuelled by colleagues who should know better. Many years ago, when 'things were different', my friend Barbarella was a recently qualified D grade doing a bit of overtime on an acute admissions psychiatric ward in the north of

England. Told to expect an admission, she prepared the bed and the forms. The patient, who was apparently well known to the regular staff, arrived through the front door accompanied by two burly police officers. Apparently he had been picked up in the high street semi-naked, claiming to be the love child of a well-known current English monarch. On arrival, whilst the humourless policeman insisted on telling Barbarella that this man's bizarre and clearly unpatriotic behaviour was obviously her fault, the new patient was assessed by the doctor and put on a section two. The policemen stayed for a cup of tea. Meanwhile the patient, less than satisfied with the outcome of his mental state assessment, strolled round the familiar corridors a few times, past his favourite side room, through the canteen, out a back door down the fire exit and was out of the hospital before his escort.

Two weeks later the police phoned, in that world weary way of theirs, to say that this popular young man with a penchant for changing his name whenever it suited him had shown up at his flat and they had been called out by some vigilant warden to recapture the renegade. They phoned from the flat saying that they could not be sure of the man's identity. They got Barbarella, who was doing a lot of overtime as she was saving up for a surfboard. Barbie, who had never really seen the man properly as she had been arguing with the policemen, remembered that he often changed his name, was reluctant to be in hospital but had tattoos. The observant policemen confirmed that he did have tattoos. Barbarella checked with the regular staff who said something like, 'Oh it's him all right,' based on what, we don't know, but who was she to question? So she said, 'That's him all right, him with the tattoos and the keys to his own flat,' so despite the man's protestations he was brought in.

On arrival of course it transpired that the man was a neighbour charged with feeding the goldfish of the Queen's love child. He was unimpressed, the police were unimpressed, and Barbarella, embarrassed by the error and struck by the invisibility of her colleagues, never surfed again. Such is the difficulty of being a D grade nurse.

But there is a beauty to it as well. This is the place where you get to make all the things you have learnt, all the things you have come to believe, happen. Where you begin to develop the confidence and experience to nurse in the style of you. You find out more about yourself in the first year of being a qualified nurse than at any other time in your life. What you are good at, what you are bad at, to what extent your menstrual cycle or your capacity to contain a hangover affects your ability to nurse well. You will begin to find out why you like some patients more than others and how to hide such things. You will work with people who die and others who make remarkable recoveries. You will find that there are small things, unseen, skilful, bits of irreducible nursing, that change the world for your patient and make your day more worthwhile, more alive, than you can describe.

I'm wondering at this point if I impressed upon you how important it is that you release the pony. Please, whatever you do, don't pretend to release the pony but keep it in a field somewhere where the fences are just a little bit too high for the little fellah to jump over. That is just too cruel. I know that you love your pony and I know you are very grateful to your parents for buying it for you, but let the pony go. I would estimate that there are perhaps 150 000 D grade nurses in the country. If only half of you have parents who bought you a pony when you qualified that is 75 000 unnecessarily restrained ponies. Set them free. You know it makes sense. There are few sights quite as moving as seeing a herd of liberated ponies trotting through town on their way to the shops to buy their little pony consumables with their little pony money in their little pony purses. Please, I implore you: let the ponies go.

In olden days, unless you were unlucky, you didn't tend to stay at D grade for long. It was always supposed to be an almost transitional grade. It was where you translated knowledge and uncertainty into practice and confidence. These days however many of you get 'stuck' there for five years and more. Of course this is unfair. There is nothing wrong with being a D grade but chances are that after a while you are all doing the job of an E grade on D grade wages. Sometimes you may find yourself running the ward, staffed by agency nurses, health care assistants and the irritatingly supernumerary students who may bother you with unmet learning objectives whilst you try to nurse.

There are perhaps two elements to being stuck on a D grade. One is simply the pay and the other is an issue of respect. It is reasonable to expect that if you nurse well and consistently at the sharp end of care, then you should be afforded the respect of having that labour recognised. However, because of the internal market and all those silly contracts, not only are there restrictions to promotional opportunity but there is seemingly nobody who can take responsibility for that restraint. The charge nurse or team leader's hands are tied by the contract manager, whose hands are tied by the contract she manages, which is negotiated by faceless people who are overpaid and unable to think of the consequences for nurses of the choices they feel compelled to make. Let's assume that everyone is doing the best they can to make health care work. If health care still doesn't work it doesn't take a genius to conclude that if the people who run the system are not failing then the system itself has.

On the other hand there are one or two nurses for whom it is perhaps best that they stay a while at D grade. Barbarella tells of an experience from her time in acute psychiatry. It is not unusual for acute admission wards to be completely full; in fact they often operate at 125% capacity. This obviously means juggling with the beds of patients on weekend leave and booking out other patients to neighbouring wards when an emergency admission is expected.

One Friday evening, with her ward full and overflowing, Barbie was told to expect another admission via casualty. She had no option but to try to transfer a patient to a less intensive bed. She phoned the rehabilitation ward and spoke to someone we shall call Alan.

'Do you have a vacant bed?' she asked.

'Hang on.' Alan wandered off to ask his charge nurse and returned to say, 'Yes we have one.'

'Good,' she said, 'we are expecting a new admission so we need it. I'll arrange the transfer and send someone down.'

'No need,' said the helpful Alan, 'I'll sort it out,' and duly hung up.

Of course Barbie was touched by the generous offer of help but had no idea how Alan was going to inform the patient of the need to transfer him, do the paper work, sort out his prescription and arrange for a nurse to go with the patient to his new ward and offer a handover. She asked a colleague to talk to the patient and arrange to take him down to the rehab ward. Under the circumstances the patient was very helpful. So often an unfair expectation is placed on patients who are supposed to be in a safe, supportive and consistent environment. However, shortly after the patient and the nurse left the ward, they bumped into Alan, wheeling a bed towards them.

'Where are you going with that?' they asked.

'Barbarella asked for a spare bed,' he replied, 'but we want it back by Monday.'

'Nurse?' asked the patient, 'How were you going to get it up the stairs?'

So quickly moving on from the occasional fool, you may notice that now you are a qualified nurse, doing all that competent stuff to do with people's health, your friends and acquaintances may view you in a different way. Firstly if you are at a party or out yachting or abseiling or whatever you young people do these days, you can rest assured that your very presence cultivates a sense of safety among your non-nursing colleagues.

Even I have experienced this and I'm not even a proper nurse, merely an RMN. I remember once being in the middle of town on a little shopping trip when, quite out of the blue, a herd of stampeding ponies started charging toward us. Of course it wasn't a complete surprise, we'd seen the ponies hanging around the town centre earlier and we thought they had been drinking. They had vaguely insulted a few passers by and had whistled at some girl ponies who were on their lunch break, having got Saturday jobs in Boots. But we hadn't imagined a stampede. What does a herd of stampeding ponies look like? Well I'm sorry but I didn't stop to take any photos.

'What should we do Mark?' asked a frightened friend who works in advertising.

'How the hell should I know?' I shouted, heading for the pony pen in the pet shop. I figured that's the last place they would go.

'You're a bloody nurse!' he shouted accusingly.

Which I think illustrates my point. People expect you to have all the answers.

Even now I have the occasional journalist come up to me and say:

'My leg hurts.'

'Why's that then?'

'You tell me, you're a nurse.' And of course I have no idea, but I may guess.

'You've probably been sitting funny.'

'Yeah that'll be it. Thanks'.

You see, you reassure people. Unfortunately this can become a bit of a responsibility. If for example you are in the park with several non-nurses and a game of Frisbee develops, invariably and with little prompting it is you who feels responsible for organising the game. Picking the sides, testing the Frisbee, making sure everybody gets to have the same amount of throws; maybe devising a little league for everyone and using your penknife to carve small prizes for all the Frisbee throwers regardless of their Frisbee ability. It just becomes part of your nature to look after everyone.

The second manifestation is that unlike just about all other jobs, people expect you to want to practice it at all times. If you meet someone and tell them you are a nurse then invariably they feel compelled to tell you something that you have to nurse. They tend to see this as doing you a favour, as if you just can't wait to nurse and the greatest gift they, a complete stranger, can give you is someone to nurse. They tell you about their sore heads, dodgy backs, erectile dysfunctions (you can rest assured that this line of conversation is rarely used as a chat-up line). They want you to feel affirmed. God forbid you ever want to talk about anything else.

You think this doesn't happen to mental health nurses?

'Hello, what do you do?'

'I'm a nurse, but before you tell me about your dizzy spells or your musical bowels I should tell you I am a mental health nurse.'

'Mental health eh? I get really depressed sometimes. And occasionally I think the trees talk to me, well whistle, when I go by anyway.'

Or worse, you get the 'I'm mad me!' brigade.

' ... You could write a book about me mate. I'm mad, bonkers! You know what my mates call me? Mad Mike!'

'Is your name Mike?'

'No. That's how mad I am. Sometimes, right, I go out in the winter wearing just a T-shirt!'

'Does that make you mad or merely northern?'

'It's not just that, I do all kinds of mad things ...'

And the man who is not Mike starts banging his head quite hard with a large tin of biscuits.

This does not happen to other professions. You may meet an accountant at a party and you may even choose to talk to him but if you asked him some advice about accounting it would be with embarrassment not glee. You would certainly not rush up to him and say, 'Offshore accounts, an appropriate financial choice for a middle-income family or not?'

If you met a policeman you wouldn't feel compelled to start confessing to your complete lack of a TV license or the sweets you stole from the corner shop in 1967. The chances are that you would expect anyone who did any job in the world to be perfectly able and more than willing to talk about something other than their job, but this is not the case with nurses. Nursing, for its sins is imagined still to be something of a vocation. Those who nurse crave the nursing role at all times and are never off duty.

Welcome to the job. If you don't watch yourself it may just screw you up.

The 'E' Grade

◆ ◆ ◆ ◆ ◆ ◆ ◆

As the fluffy little Tamla songstress Diana Ross once said: 'You are everything and everything is you.' And the chances are she was thinking of E grade staff nurses across the United Kingdom as she said it. Of course there are those pop historians who suggest that she was thinking of Marvin Gaye, but I prefer to believe that she was thinking of you. I can say with some certainty that if my application to be on Stars In Their Eyes is successful, and Matthew asks me, 'Who are you going to be tonight, Mark?' I'll reply, 'Tonight, Matthew, I'm going to be Diana Ross!' And when I go on to sing that delightful ditty, I will be thinking of you. However, having said that, I was planning to do 'Ain't no mountain high enough'.

Anyway despite the undoubted greatness of Marvin Gaye he did sing 'The world is just a great big onion' which is at best misleading and at worst a great big lie. So I don't think Diana would be singing about Marvin, I think she would be singing to you. I'm glad that's sorted.

As an E grade you will have to do just about everything. You will be the named nurse, the primary nurse, the nurse in charge of shifts, the nurse who has to do those silly ENB courses and the nurse who organises the tea kitty. We'll come back to this, and I don't mean the tea kitty.

As you are the substantial body of nursing's workforce, I'm curious about how you want nursing to be referred to. Is it a profession or a job? A craft? A social science? An art or an activity? I tend to think of nursing as an activity. A weightless term with no pretension or meaningful history. The whole 'professionalisation' of nursing strikes me as one of the most stupid wastes of time I have come across since a friend of mine chose to spend a year organising all of his spoken sentences into alphabetical order, such was his penchant for regulation. Thus a grey day would be described as 'another big cloud descends – everyone, forget going hiking.' My friend is a social worker.

Perhaps E grade is the place where the nature of nursing really comes home to roost. The activities of your day are less likely to contain surprises. You are not on a constant voyage of discovery. Of course there will still be the new experience. The patient who can only describe his moods by relating them to lowly or highly rated football teams:

'Can you shave today?'

'Oh no, I can't shave today. I'm Swindon Town.'

Or 'You seem a bit happier today, it's nice to see you smiling.'

'Today I'm Chelsea.'

But in the main, one of the transitions you make at E grade is from managing the unusual to sustaining the incessant. Perhaps the most profound expenditure you will make will be emotional. How are you going to manage the feelings you collect, the emotional demands that are made on you and the sometimes extreme feelings of sadness, loss, anger or guilt, however irrational they are, that you are left with?

There will be all sorts of formal arrangements that your chosen work environment will provide for you here. Clinical supervision, support days, generous annual leave entitlement, little unexpected presents, free sweets, professional recognition. You may get a little plaque for example. Sometimes your manager may come round after work and help you with the ironing. There are so many ways that you will be supported and thanked. But still you may need more.

One of the problems with being a nurse is the ridiculous pressure placed on you by an unthinking society and the collusive unimaginative professional bodies for you to live and breathe nursing. This is a nonsense. It is far healthier to get out and do other things whenever possible. You know it, I know it. It's only fools who imagine that you want to spend your spare time studying more nursing or thinking of better ways of nursing or simply doing overtime to pay your mortgage. Personally I'm a big fan of studying, but I have never studied, nor will I ever study, nursing. Nursing is simply what I did and will no doubt do again, it's not what I need to study. If you are going to study, study something energising, balancing, that's what I say. Scuba dive or learn how to tattoo people (a word of warning here, when practising your tattooing skills always try to get the consent of your subject before or at least during the actual tattooing process).

Daniel, a part-time lover of Barbarella's, has been a nurse for 13 years. He has worked in HIV and AIDS for most of that time. He is not a big fan of the rather trite courses available to him professionally and has thus chosen to stimulate himself in other ways. At first he just did short courses in things that he considered interesting and where he might meet different people. He learnt how to parachute, which he claimed was not as difficult as we might imagine. Basically, he said, you get in a plane, wait for it to take off – that's important apparently – open the door, first ensuring that you are wearing a parachute, jump out and pull the cord. His first attempt was a bit of a failure because he got on the wrong plane. Fortunately the stewardess on the 737 en route to Corfu sensed he was no ordinary holidaymaker because although he took full advantage of the duty free bar he insisted on standing beside the exit wearing borrowed goggles with what looked like a tent strapped to his back. The silly sausage.

The next time he got the plane right and the jump went pretty much as he planned except he landed on his bottom, which serves him right for missing the last lesson whilst lounging around in Corfu.

However his love of danger went unabated. Next he started a part-time degree in dance. Now Daniel is a lovely little mover but at 26, smoking 30 a day and being a shade porky he was perhaps at a bit of a disadvantage when measured against the chocolate-shunning 17-year-olds who had been springing about like Nureyev since they were two, but he was nothing if not game. He managed two years of the degree, whilst still working shifts and smoking and eating the packed lunches of his 46 fellow students before an unfortunate misinterpretation in the otherwise beautiful Swan Lake led to his departure. In fairness Daniel maintains that he probably offered a more than legitimate interpretation of Tchaikovsky's work when he shot the swan and sat on all the cygnets 15 minutes in. 'All that springing about can puff you out,' he argued, but his tutor, and less surprisingly perhaps the maimed swan, felt otherwise and it was time for Daniel to move on.

Next he tried physics. Why, we all asked. Because he wanted to find out about space and time, he said. What shape is space, for example, and whether Einstein's theory – that if you took off in a rocket at ten to five and travelled for a fortnight at the speed of light and returned to the same place it would be still be ten to five especially if your watch had stopped – made any sense. If it was true would he still age? If he could pull it off could he have two girlfriends? And most pertinently what kind of drugs was Einstein taking? Like most people studying physics Daniel lasted about a week but did some dandy doodles in his specially purchased physics notepad with a picture of Mr Spock on it. And so he moved on again.

In his time Daniel studied still life drawing, glass painting, Chinese philosophy, fencing and jewellery making. (It is a sociological fact that if just half the number of people who insist on making crap jewellery would get their ears pierced then at least some might stand a chance of selling some of their beaded nonsense.)

Finally Daniel found something he loved: languages. He took a combined degree in Spanish, French and Linguistics, and remains to this day the only man I know who thinks linguistics is interesting.

Has it helped him nurse? Absolutely. He can speak to hospital managers in French and Spanish which hacks them off sometimes but makes him laugh. But more importantly he was having a great time. Except perhaps for the physics. Anything that enlivens must be healthy, especially if you are giving so much of yourself in your job. Which brings us back to PREP and first those funny little ENB courses.

Now, I don't know who the ENB is or the WNB or the NBS or any other NB. I'm sure they are perfectly nice people living perfectly nice lives. However one suspects that they are living these perfectly nice lives in a village where it is still 1934. The air is rarefied, and nobody has to lock their door when they go out in ENB town. The population gathers its understanding of the world from a dusty wireless in the church hall and on a Saturday evening families congregate to hear Bing Crosby crooning. Everyone who lives in

ENB town has far too many names. Mr and Mrs Woodley-Gaze for example, and the family Tetra Von Block. But they love nursing, and they have their finger on a pulse.

The inhabitants of ENB town, like so many of us, carry within them the eternal struggle between instinct and intellect. They are not unlike the mild mannered Bruce Wayne in that respect. On the one hand a billionaire businessman with a nice old butler and a friend called Dick, but on the other a dark avenging knight with the instincts of a bat and a caped mate called Robin. The instincts of ENB town are the instincts of 1934. Nurses are lovely gals, pretty little whippets, none too bright but spunky in an English Rose kind of way. However, their unsurprisingly failing intellects suggest that it is not 1934, despite the obvious popularity of Crosby and tweed waistcoats, and the world outside the town dances to a different rhythm. Out there, nurses are a body of highly skilled people who require constant education and professional regulation. So the masters of ENB town came up with a series of courses to help the feisty little vixens along in their funny modern ways. Unfortunately the courses they have devised are, and I mean this in a positive way, absolute crap.

Take the experience of Daniel.

'Would you like to go on a course young Daniel?' the nice squires of AIDS care suggested.

'That would be smashing,' said the experienced Daniel, who has been working in HIV for seven years. 'I would like something that would help me to re-appraise the way I cope with the seeming incessance of death. To perhaps re-evaluate from a slightly world-weary perspective how I can continue to nurse well. I would like, and I think would benefit from, the opportunity of sharing and listening to the experiences of other nurses who have worked extensively in this area. Maybe explore how we deal with what is for me the hardest thing in nursing, looking into the eyes of parents who are watching their children die and just don't understand. I have never been able to spend time with those parents who expect, indeed pray, to die before their children, without going home and crying.'

'Right, we have such a course,' said Farquar-Thomas who had handily arrived from ENB town. 'However, you can't do it because in order to do ENB 280 you must first do ENB 934: Introduction to caring for patients with AIDS.'

And so Daniel got to do 934 and when asked at the end of the course to feed back what he had learnt, he said honestly, 'Well, nothing, thank you. It seems the thrust of the course is that AIDS can be nasty, watch out, and frankly I'd pretty much picked that up.' The tutors, all of whom had several ENB courses under their belts including, 763: Nursing: good isn't it?, and 512: Appropriate fastening of sensible shoes in advanced clinical practice, were less than enamoured with Daniel's clear denial of the appropriateness and brilliance of their beloved course and they did not give him many ticks. Still he got his certificate which is the main thing apparently.

And of course there is ENB 998. Now it's easy for me to criticise for I do not have the 998. I was offered it four times during my post-registration nursing career. Each time I asked why I would want to do a course that replicates everything that one does in one's training, I was told, 'It's good to have it though.' Finally when I was a G grade I was told that I was the only G grade in the community mental health teams who did not have the 998 and yet, because I was running a walk-in service as opposed to working independently in the community, I had more students than any of my colleagues.

You may remember this momentous occasion because the whole planet tilted from its axis, the rains came, the wonderful symmetry that is nature began to weep and the heavens opened, large trees fell and small houses were whisked away by God's ill will. Geri Gingerperson left the Spice Girls and the omnibus edition of Coronation Street did not appear on Sunday. Yet somehow we survived. You can have no more students, they said, for you are not qualified to teach them. 'Neither are their teachers,' I said, 'judging by how the poor sods feel by the time they get here.' The students kept coming and my misguided distaste was forgotten. There are few things more pointless than ENB 998. Waiting at bus stops, perhaps, re-runs of Dad's Army, that stupid video of Queen singing Bohemian Rhapsody; but beyond that, very very little.

Most of the ENB courses are pointless and out of touch. Still to their credit they are cheap and easy and that makes them useful in the face of PREP.

PREP is probably a very fine idea in principle. Yes, facilitate on-going training and education for nurses; yes, even institutionalise it so that the provision of new learning is made implicit in a nurse's career. Educational opportunity for nurses is good. So long as they get the money, space, time and appropriate freedom of choice to pursue their education. But its introduction has been thoughtless: it's as though someone said, 'We need to introduce PREP to nurses; it will help us appear committed to regulation and education. Take this really big bucket and bring back a load of thought that we can use for its presentation.' And the person they sent forgot the bloody bucket and so he had to fill his pockets with thought, but he had really little trousers on and his small trousers had holes, so essentially there wasn't much thought.

Consequently PREP has arrived and it doesn't look like an opportunity, it looks like a big scary space monster that is going to lose people their jobs. Those are the worst big ugly space monsters by the way. Don't worry too much about the ones that growl and look like they are going to eat you or get slime on you that turns you into an alien or something. The big ugly space monsters you really have to look out for are the ones that make you lose your job.

There are thousands and thousands of nurses who understandably consider PREP to be one more hurdle in the great steeplechase of nursing. They have to find appropriate courses or bits of study; they feel unsure of how best to demonstrate that on-going learning is happening. Most alarmingly, they partly expect some kind of grey-suited hit-squad to appear on their doorstep in the middle of the night and demand to see their portfolio, and they would have to answer the door in their jammies and say, 'He doesn't live here,' and the evil UKCC bureaucrats would say, 'No, not Portillo; portfolio.' And if the poor jammied nurses don't have their portfolios they would fear being dragged off to UKCC headquarters where they would have their fob watches ceremoniously removed and thereupon be cast out into the night and labelled as really bad girls!

Won't happen. Firstly people who work for the UKCC are not allowed to travel anywhere together in case something terrible happens, like they are involved in an accident and thus the UKCC is left understaffed and maybe on the brink of destruction and consequently the whole fabric of nursing is threatened. Because let's face it, we couldn't possibly go on without them. Another bad thing that might happen is that if they go out in pairs or small UKCC grouplets they might start asking each other difficult questions like, 'What's the point of us again?' or, 'How many other professions have to pay to carry on working?' until finally one of the sobbing bureaucrats screams, 'And another thing. The Code of Conduct – it's bollocks isn't it?'

Secondly, we can pretty much turn PREP into what we want. It is merely about continuing to learn, essentially institutionalising the same processes that have always existed in nursing. But PREP makes it more official and the posh people can boast about regulation and professional status.

If you read an article, that counts as PREP; if you talk reflectively or constructively about work, that's PREP. If you take any kind of course, do any kind of thinking or writing, that is PREP. So there's no need to worry about PREP.

The real disgustingly irritating thing about PREP however is the assumption that people who actually do the nursing (that is, not those who write about it, or make pompous policies about it or pronounce nonsense on it, but the people who just kind of do it) are expected to use their own time and money, and that is taking advantage. If the powers that be want nursing to be austere, regulated and professional then they ought to facilitate their funny little inventions with proper finance and a political commitment to decent wages.

It may be the case that E grade is the place where the final metamorphosis takes place from considerate person to caring professional. Of course you may still be a considerate person and that will no doubt shine through, in fact it may still be your emotional and intellectual motivator, but in terms of 'doing caring' at people it is not possible to rely on your beautiful nature. In fact by the time you are this far into your working life it would not be healthy.

Nursing teaches you how to care systematically. You use your professionalism prior to using your capacity for human concern. If you did not you, the human being, would swell up into a big watery bag of other people's distress. If you don't know this by the time you are an E grade you are either a saint or you are likely to burst, creating a nasty slimy mess on the floor. Most nurses, whether we like it or not, have learnt this. This fact is proven beyond all doubt by the relative lack of stories in the papers about nurses bursting like blisters all over the place and leaking, seeping even, on to hospital floors. Maybe popped nurses would raise few concerns but the infection control implications are far reaching.

Of course there were one or two stories earlier this year, you may remember the headlines: 'Nurse spontaneously splatters passengers on bus, following particularly hard day'; 'She ruined my trousers says doctor who stood by whilst nurse detonated'; and from the Sun 'Blimey! Slimy Kylie spurty nursey', which pretty much says it all. But in the main, by the time you are an E grade you have professionalised your way of caring. You are clear about your personal boundaries and you probably won't detonate.

But for those of you who are still worried that you may splatter, here are a few tips, gathered from E grade colleagues, that may help you avoid unsightly emotional seepage.

1. When you are at a party, or round your boyfriend's mother's house, and people start telling you about their needs as if you were born to nurse and only nurse and may well shrivel up or expire if someone does not give you something to nurse every three hours, don't nurse them. Do not remotely nurse them. I know sometimes it's easier to slip into something like autopilot and make the right noises and 'ooh' and 'aah' and stuff, but once you start you will

never stop. You will forever be your boyfriend's mum's little helper. I'm not going to suggest that you make a big speech about how you are more than a mere nurse, in fact you are a woman, with your own hopes and dreams ... etc. Just say something like, 'Ooh that sounds nasty, you ought to see someone about that.'

2. Get yourself a little hobby.

3(a). Have a family. There is nothing like a significant other, or children or whatever, to re-prioritise your life. The nurses with families always strike me as the well-balanced ones. It looks terribly impressive and grown-up. Or,

3(b). Replace the stability and love of family life with the vain and seemingly purposeless pursuit of excess. Experiment with life; party, have a string of lovers ... yes it's tiring, but it takes your mind off work, apparently.

4. Take occasional breaks from work, if at all possible. Holidays are good, and courses are useful ways of just being in a different place. I always used to take a month off between jobs. Mind you I had low rent and no dependants.

5. Find a way of occasionally laughing with your colleagues. I know it's hard, I know sometimes your colleagues may not like to laugh, especially if they are physiotherapists for example. Picnics are good, except not in November; pubs are very therapeutic places for nurses (but then you know that). Laughing at the world, at yourself and at the doctors is a very good way of avoiding seepage.

Of course it is quite possible that you planned your career meticulously from an early age, deciding when you were seven for example that you were going to specialise in Cognitive Behavioural Therapy. Or you could have stumbled into it without a grand plan, more a vague inclination towards something genuinely challenging, and found yourself nursing. You may only now be thinking about what direction your career is likely to take.

Market research suggests that there are three types of nurses. Now before we go any further we should remember that we are talking about people who work in market research here so it would be best not to expect too much sophistication. However the three types of nurse are high-flyers, coasters and sidelined nurses.

The high-flyers are the ones with an eye for the top. They plan their careers meticulously and engage with the professional world with a systematic zeal that makes the SAS look like the Woodentops.

The second group, the coasters, pretty much, well, coast actually. They are likely to have young families and invest more in home life, require flexibility in their work and may try to develop their careers dependent on the age and needs of their children.

Finally, there are the sidelined nurses. The ones who basically nurse, often at E or G grade for some time. They have no desire to develop their careers. They may be vaguely disdainful, unaware or simply and coolly uninterested in the machinations of modern nursing.

I know it's wrong to have favourites but I like the sidelined nurses. They are definitely the ones who go behind the bikesheds at play time. If John Travolta was a nurse he would be a sidelined nurse. Sidelined nurses are cool. High-flyers, bless them, are not cool; they always look like they are trying and that is only ever attractive in very small children.

As an E grade you probably have a pretty good idea about which of these three groups you are in. You are, perhaps, faced with having to think about your career development. Horrible isn't it?

Let's be honest here: career development is dependent on several interlacing factors and they are not the same factors that you were told about during your training. These factors include:

1. Being good at what you do. This often helps but not always. I once worked with an E grade, for example, whom I would not have trusted with the kettle let alone the clients. Six months ago he was promoted to G grade. I mentioned to former colleagues that unless he had undergone a remarkable transformation such a promotion was ludicrous, adding that if they had no other candidates I had a pen top that could do the job better. They said they had already considered the pen top possibility but he had apparently applied for about 3000 jobs in the previous year and they felt they could not say no again. They worried that he might complain about equal opportunities or something. However in the

main we have to believe that being good at your job counts for something, otherwise we find ourselves living in a completely and indefensibly corrupt world and that would be too much to bear.

2. Desire. At the very least this is a double-edged sword (still don't know what that means). Either you will need to really want to get on, to fill that senior or specialist post because you feel you could do it better than anyone else or that the post will motivate and nourish you. And it may be the case that you were born to run. Having said that, when Springsteen wrote his escapist rock anthem I don't think he was thinking of a nurse practitioner post, although this depends on how you interpret the second verse.

Or you will need to possess the other form of desire, common but rarely spoken of, the desire NOT to be doing whatever it is you are doing. Perfectly legitimate, this one. Life decisions are often based not on where one wants to get to but rather where one wants to leave.

3. Charm and articulacy. Yes I know it shouldn't matter but we all know it does. If, and I realise this is unlikely, you find yourself eating your dinner with someone who may have power over your future, make sure you use your cutlery (this constitutes charm), and if he asks how you would save money on the nurse budget be articulate in your response. Manager types love free-flowing answers to pointless questions; it is the manager equivalent of potential. Don't worry about content, by the way – that's the last thing managers tend to look for.

4. Being in the right place at the right time. Also known as opportunism. But remember there is a difference between finding yourself ideally located to slip unopposed into your dream job and finding yourself standing behind someone who is ideally located for your ideal job and setting fire to them.

OK, that's enough lists. Most people say that their time as an E grade was their happiest time as a nurse. Mind you lots of people say that your schooldays are the best days of your life, which is patently ridiculous. However in lots of ways E grade nursing is the heart of the experience and the most nourishing of places to work from. You get to do some really good clinical work, and to individualise your care. You get to flourish in terms of style and impact and the core of your day is about patient contact, which is the best bit. You know your patients and they know you. And you nurse.

It may be the case that one is not allowed to talk of the activity of nursing, its power and the millions of illustrations that demonstrate it. It may be that our age is so ironic or evidence-based that tales from the everyday experience strike us as twee or embarrassing. However, if the language that surrounds, pervades and perhaps offends nursing is always in the form of smug commentary or pseudo-science, we may just lose the plot. That, then, is my excuse for the following.

A friend called Sam had a friend called Samantha. They worked together as E grades in the north of England on a rehabilitation ward for the older person. They both recall a patient called Mr Smith. Mr Smith was dying and he wanted to die at home. His daughter, a devoted woman who had cared for him for some time, wanted him to die at home. One of the primary reasons for his hospitalisation were two gaping infected wounds in his buttocks that went through to his hips. Sam and Samantha, and another E grade called Cindy, rarely worked on the same shifts, but they all worked with Mr Smith.

They nursed well, the way nurses can and usually do, and they compared notes. Sam reports that he felt he was engaged in a partnership with his fellow nurse, his patient and his patient's daughter. Soon the wounds had healed enough for Mr Smith to go home.

After a few weeks Mr Smith's daughter rang Sam and told him that the wounds were worsening and she could not get the materials to dress them, nor did she have the skill and nor did she feel able to work with any of the other services for various reasons.

Now as we all know, rules are rules. But sometimes it's best to bend them. Sam took some dressing packs from the ward, went round to Mr Smith's house and worked with his daughter, teaching her to dress the wounds. A week later Samantha went round and did the same. The wounds were controlled.

A couple of months later Mr Smith died. His daughter invited Sam and Samantha to the funeral. They attended. There was hugging involved. Sam said that he felt he was nursing the family by nursing the wounds; that everything clicked.

Yes, it's an everyday story, far from outstanding or myth making but that's the point. Nursing is everyday stories and we are in danger of forgetting the resonance of everyday stories because they are not dramatic enough or different enough. The culture of the remarkable has perhaps overtaken us and as a consequence we could lose everything without even noticing.

Sam, Samantha and their friend Cindy all worked together on that ward for about two years. They all went their separate ways, mainly because if you keep getting jobs in small groups people get suspicious.

Daniel meantime reports working over a long period in an HIV care setting with someone called Alan who had anaemia. Alan confessed to Daniel that he had had hundreds of blood transfusions and their purpose had been explained to him dozens of times, but he really didn't get it. Daniel explained that essentially blood was a 30-truck haulage firm and anaemia was the equivalent of having 10 lorries out of operation and some emergency haulage to do. It became a running joke but Alan got the point.

Some time later, shortly after Alan had died, the nurses found a poem that he had written, in appreciation of them. The fact that he had taken the time to think of them was touching, the fact that he appreciated them meant the world.

As for the triumvirate of Cindy, Sam and Samantha, Cindy became a wound care specialist, and has been running a ward very happily for the last eight years. Samantha became something academic, winning lots of prizes for her clever ways and knowing the answers to loads of questions. Sam set up a new rehab ward and went on to wander the world of nursing, righting wrongs wherever he found them. They all say that their time on that ward, and the team they were part of was the best job they ever had.

THE 'F' GRADE

◆ ◆ ◆ ◆ ◆ ◆ ◆

F GRADE DIARY
MON 5 Swiss rolls
3 gins
TUES 2 Kit Kats
20 cigs (bad)
WEDS ½ bottle wine
0 cigs (good)
THURS 3 Wagon Wheels
FRI 3 Gins
2 Kit Kats
25 Cigs (help!)

Nancy Kite, friend, royalist, junior sister. Nancy is a woman of many talents. She can wrestle like a man, a skill she picked up watching the grapple and groan on a Saturday afternoon and then practising on the sofa or her father. She can juggle, she can do little mosaics. She is, in short, more than just a nurse.

Nancy is new to her F grade. Indeed, quite unusually she has progressed rather rapidly through the ranks, assisted along the way by her dedicated sense of professionalism, her degree in media studies and her admirable ambition. Nancy is by no means a typical F grade. But then, who the hell is? However she has her sights set high and she dreams of one day running her own aseptic kingdom. Here are a few extracts from her diary, offered by Nancy in an effort to share the complex and irreducible experience of nursing.

Friday 15th August

Still no sign of Sister Mercy retiring. Perhaps it's a bit too much to hope for, her being 32 and fit as a fiddle. But I can't help thinking that one day all this will be mine. In the meantime I will continue to leave adverts for timeshare apartments laying around her office.

Had plain yoghurt and a banana for lunch. Very disciplined, have lost six ounces this week. Celebrate with a Crunchie. Put on a pound and it went straight to my hips. Sister Mercy ate a big plate of chips and about a yard of lasagne, followed by treacle pudding and custard and some crisps. I also noticed that she had three Hobnobs with her tea. She should be the size of a bungalow but instead looks like Michele Pfeiffer. I hate Sister Mercy although she has always been good to me. She has to be – this ward would crumble without me.

New admission this afternoon. Kidney stones they said, but I had my doubts. She looked to me like the sort who takes drugs. She had her ears pierced and everything. Instructed the other nurses to keep an eye on her. I am unsure as to what exactly it is I have to do as an F grade but it may be to play moral guardian.

Am going to the pictures tomorrow with Andrew. Our first date. He is a mental health nurse so I'll have to pay my own admission.

I met him on a management course last week. He seemed nice with good teeth, but I shall reserve judgement. I am on an early tomorrow so early night.

Particularly gripping episode of Emmerdale. There are clearly more lesbians in that programme than there are in the whole of the West Midlands. We don't have lesbians in the West Midlands. There was a girl at my school who drank beer and liked metalwork, but I think it was just a phase.

Saturday 16th August

The drug-taking reprobate with so-called kidney stones is a vegetarian, which pretty much confirms my suspicions. She is almost certainly an enemy of the state who did not sign the Princess Diana Queen of Hearts memorial book. However I am a professional and will rise above the understandable distaste she arouses in me. Not like that nice Mr Fodder-Chapman in bed nine. He's certainly upstanding, or at least he was when I gave him a bed bath yesterday.

The date with Andrew was not a big success. He smokes, which is going to have to stop before he kisses me and I believe he may have a tattoo. However he took me to see Wuthering Heights with Laurence Olivier and Merle Toblerone, which is based on a song by Kate Bush. He said I had an ironic sense of humour which threw me. I said I was a junior sister and I didn't have a sense of humour. And he laughed, the cheeky monkey. He too is an F grade.

Sister Mercy looked a bit peaky.

Sunday 17th August

The enemy of the state said she wanted to go home. Was surprised to hear she had a home. Had come to believe that she lived under the arches, not that I know where the arches are. Apparently she claims to be a nurse, which for some reason made some of the other staff a little nervous. All the more reason to ignore her I say. Everyone knows that nurses are the worst patients, or at least they get treated the worst. Anyway if she is a nurse she should know how busy we are. I investigated whilst checking her blood pressure. She can't be a very good nurse, she can't even spell diastolic.

Mr Fodder-Chapman had a female visitor. I think it was his sister although Sister Mercy had to tell them that all visitors are requested to keep at least one foot on the floor when saying hello to the patients. She also remarked that it is preferred that they keep their bras on. I think Mr Fodder-Chapman likes me.

Sister Mercy is planning a holiday. I said I would bring in some adventure brochures and urged her to try white-water rafting and bungee jumping.

Had a tomato for my dinner, and half a sausage for my tea. Lost four ounces. Celebrated with trifle. Went straight to just one hip and am in danger of looking a little lop-sided. Will redouble my efforts to lose weight tomorrow.

Tuesday 19th August

Junior Staff Nurse Sarah Burton-West is almost definitely after my job, the big fat cow! During the staff support group Sister Mercy asked us all where we see ourselves in a year's time and Sarah said that she hoped to be an F grade by then. She just came right out and said it as if I wasn't even there! And the new girl Veronica Bake she said she wanted an E grade within 18 months, she's only been qualified five minutes! I said that I was happy as I was but that I would like to one day run my own ward. Sister Mercy said she was very happy that so many of her staff were ambitious and hard working but I imagine that really she was shocked by the feeding frenzy that is modern nursing. Sister Mercy also told us that we had a new staff nurse coming and he was a boy. Veronica Bake blushed as she does every time she hears the word boy. My own view is that if God had wanted boys to nurse he would have given them smaller hands, but I am adaptable.

The drug-crazed pinko vegetarian is still with us. She had a visitor today and I certainly did not authorise the mother of the enemy of the state to bring in cake! God alone knows what ingredients went into it but that didn't stop Sarah Burton-West having about five slices. The two ends of Sarah's belt are complete strangers. I don't think old so-called kidney stones girl is too enamoured with our care. I'm tempted to tell her to go to Russia and see what care she gets there except of course Russia is on our side now so I keep schtum.

Sister Mercy surprisingly finds a pile of job adverts on her desk.

Thursday 21st August

The doctors said that the vegetarian who has been feigning agony since she got here has the worst case of kidney stones they have ever seen and increase her pain control. Sarah Burton-West, who incidentally has far too many names for one person, asks me if I feel bad about all the horrible things I said about her. I say I don't because it didn't affect my professionalism, and remind myself that at some point soon we really ought to ask her her name, and maybe cobble together a care plan or something.

Friday 22nd August

Met Andrew. He does have a tattoo. I found it strangely alluring. He suggested that I get one. I told him that would be unprofessional for a woman in my position. He laughed; he laughs a lot does Andrew.

Mr Fodder-Chapman's sister came in again, apparently she lost an earring in Mr Fodder-Chapman's pants. She asked the rotund Sarah Burton-West to help her find it. There was a lot of rustling but I did not offer to help. If Miss Burton-West is so anxious to get on so early in her career she can certainly do so without my help.

I have been thinking again of my own career. Sister Mercy, who ate a Cornetto today, shows no sign of departing and I wonder when I will have my own ward. Perhaps I should change direction. Go into the community, I've heard you get given a Fiat Uno if you work in the community but I would miss the hustle and bustle of the ward.

Saturday 23rd August

We had an emergency today. A cardiac arrest in bed five. A nice old man called Mr Wince. We brought him back, Sister Mercy and I, before the crash team arrived. It was glorious: two women working in perfect harmony. We were like Stevie Wonder's keyboard, or Starsky and Hutch – not that Starsky and Hutch were women of course, but Sister Mercy and I are too thin to be compared to Cagney and Lacey. The adrenaline was remarkable. We just couldn't calm down; it was a feeling of tireless elation. Sister Mercy and I went across the road for a drink afterwards and the rest of the staff joined us. I remember we did some singing and there may have been dancing involved. Andrew was there with a couple of other psychiatric nurses. Sister Mercy and I and Andrew and a charge nurse from his ward ended up back at Andrew's where he had tequila. I smoked a strange-smelling cigarette. Shenanigans occurred; least said, soonest mended.

Sunday 24th August

Andrew phoned. He asked if I was all right and if I wanted to talk about … what happened.

'Talk about what?' I said.

'You know,' he said.

'I don't know,' I said.

'Don't you remember?' he asked.

'Yes I remember,' I said.

'Are you sure?' he said.

'YES!' I said, 'I've got a lovebite on my calf thank you.'

'That wasn't me,' he said.

'What do you mean it wasn't you?' I said.

'I mean it wasn't me,' he said.

'But we kissed …' I said.

'Yes,' he said.

'… and continued to kiss for some time …' I said.

'Indeed,' he said.

'… and didn't we …'

'Yes,' he said. There was a pause. 'And it was very nice,' he said. 'Don't you remember?'

'Yes,' I said, 'I remember, but that's when I thought I got the lovebite on my calf.'

'No,' he said, 'that was later.'

'Not your charge nurse!' I said.

'No,' he said, 'I think it was Sister Mercy.'

'Oh my God!' I said, 'I've become Martina Navratilova.'

He laughed. 'You're really funny,' he said.

Mental health nurses are vermin. They have no scruples, they think everything is ironic. They spend all their time shrugging and smoking roll-ups.

I resolve to ask Sister Mercy if she likes Emmerdale.

The pinko, whose name was Fay or May or something, has left. Gone off to plot some kind of insurrection, no doubt. Her place is filled by a woman with exceedingly short hair and a nosestud. She does not eat the lamb cutlet presented to her at dinner time. She probably has an eating disorder.

I have trouble sleeping. I am vaguely troubled by recent events. I wonder if I may be becoming a bit of a vixen. I decide not to confront Sister Mercy.

Monday 25th August

'Sister Mercy, did you give me a lovebite on my calf?' I asked during the ward round. It's best to get these things out in the open, I decided apparently.

'Get on with your work nurse,' she said, and the consultant Dr Hedges shook his terribly well-qualified head. I'm not happy. My head hurts, my calf is scarred and I did it with Andrew. Tequila is evil and I will never touch another drop again.

Andrew has invited me to a party at the weekend. Apparently Sister Treat is going and Sarah Burton-West, so there is bound to be food. The only consolation is that the sweet trolley wheeled round every day by the friendly league of friendly friendlies has arrived early, and they have Wagon Wheels. I feel strangely compelled to eat a box of Wagon Wheels.

Sister Mercy tells me that perhaps I need a holiday and that she did not lovebite my calf.

'Sorry for asking Sister,' I said.

'Don't mention it. Oh by the way I like Andrew, he's nice and he seems rather fond of you. He says you have a dry sense of humour. You ought to bring it to work sometimes, Nancy. Laughter is a wonderful healer you know.'

This confirms for me that Sister Mercy is some kind of hippie.

Wednesday 27th August

Sister Mercy has asked me to do the off-duty for October. I could have hugged her but my calf hasn't cleared up yet. I think this is my big chance. If I can only prove to her that I can do an off-duty then soon I too will wear that nice dark-blue uniform. Perhaps she has chosen to groom me for succession. I will not let her down. I will do the best off-duty that has ever been done. All of the staff will marvel at my off-duty.

Wednesday 3rd September

This off-duty is bloody murder. I haven't slept for a week trying to sort it out. I thought I had it on Monday and I took it in to show Sister Mercy. She pointed out that I had not given Sarah Burton-West any days off in October whereas she, Sister Mercy, was only working two and a half days. Veronica Bake, who had booked two weeks off to go snowboarding in France, was doing a month of nights. The new boy Steven Oginotto was only working mornings and I had not included any requests from any of the staff.

She was very nice about it and suggested I try again and if I was having any trouble to tell her and she would help.

Friday 5th September

The off-duty is complete! And if I say so myself it's not half bad. Admittedly I have to work a 27-day stretch including four long days, but most of the other staff have had all their requests met. It is a pity that the staff don't get to vote for their favourite nurse and promote them by popular demand to G grade.

Question: When you are a Sister, do they give you your own whistle?

Monday 8th September

Great party! It turns out Sister Mercy did bite my leg but it was all done in jest. Some elaborate and clearly fetishistic drinking game the boys dreamt up. They're not so bad really, those psychiatric nurses. I wouldn't marry one, of course. They all have tattoos and strange amoral ways. Take Andrew, for example. He and I have finished. I called it all off when I found him snogging Sister Mercy. He took it well, on the outside at least. On the inside I suspect he's a broken man. His exact words were, 'Nancy, you're such a laugh,' but I think they masked a pain the size of Sarah Burton-West.

I don't know what Sister Mercy is doing kissing a man who is clearly of a lower grade than her. It confirms my hippie suspicions. Maybe this is what is known as 'a bit of rough'.

I had another of their rolly cigarettes and found myself wanting a Kit Kat more than any woman has ever wanted a Kit Kat before. Sarah, whom I think I referred to as 'man' for some strange reason, thankfully had a Rowntrees selection box in her satchel and she gave me her Kit Kat. She's not so bad, you know. It's her glands, poor love.

Tuesday 9th September

I've put on four pounds! Mr Fodder-Chapman said I looked agreeable today. And Dr Hedges. When I passed him in the corridor and nodded respectfully he didn't completely turn his head away when he ignored me, which was nice.

Emmerdale is getting really exciting. Apparently the cyborgs have got hold of the last human prophet child and are going to ritualistically slay him unless the planet Earth hands over all the world's heads of government. Without the last prophet child the earth will surely perish and so the heads of government and their families and their pets are going to sacrifice themselves for the prophet child. The only hope is the Emmerdale militia, who have a complex plan that involves a tractor.

I need a Star Bar and I need it now.

Wednesday 10th September

I was doing the drugs round today and I suddenly thought about the clouds. The big fluffy white clouds. What would it be like to walk on the clouds, hand in hand with Mr Fodder-Chapman? And the stars, I thought: 'I'd like to swing on a star, carry moonbeams home in a jar.' I may get my nipple pierced.

Had a Yorkie for dinner and some crisps. Invited Sister Mercy, Sarah and Veronica round for drinks and nibbles. Have put on another two pounds. Don't give a toss.

Thursday 11th September

We had a lovely time. Steven Oginotto came too. He is gay. Sister Mercy tells him that is a wonderful career move and the others laugh. I don't get it myself but I laugh too.

Sister Mercy is cheating on Andrew with the charge nurse who is called Ali. Sarah says she is on a diet and does not eat anything except a bit of beetroot. Veronica cries. She says that she didn't really feel accepted when she started but now she does and she loves us all. Sister Mercy says she wasn't accepted at first because she didn't seem to know what a thermometer looked like but that she has settled in nicely. I ask Sister Mercy what her first name is and she says it's Sister. I blush and wonder if I have overstepped the mark. Steven says that's a coincidence, her being a sister and all and she says she agrees but that her full title of Sister Sister Mercy is a bit annoying. I ask her if her parents had always wanted her to be a nurse and she says no, they wanted her to be a snooker player but she absolutely hated snooker. Steven said he hated my curtains and offered to run me up some nice new ones. He has small hands for a man.

Sister Mercy tells me that I seem a bit tense sometimes. I take the little cigarette from her fingers and tell her that I'm not tense; I'm actually a fun-loving criminal, but I'm trying to live up to my responsibilities, whatever the hell they are. I try to prove my lack of tension by doing my Norman Wisdom impression but instead I go all giggly like a demented vole. I wonder why my giggling makes me think of voles. I wouldn't know a vole if someone put one down my pants. I giggle even more because I thought of the word pants and I tend to only think of the word pants when I am on a date, doing the ironing or about to be struck by a speeding car.

Giggle so much I almost wet myself. Tell Sister Mercy I will wet myself if she does not get me a box of Terry's All Gold.

Friday 12th September

Steven tells me he likes the Bee Gees and I like the Bee Gees! He likes to do mosaics and I do mosaics! I like Steven.

Saturday 13th September

Steven comes round to my house with my new curtains. They're lovely. We get talking, and it turns out he likes wrestling and has a signed photograph of Kendo Nagasaki. I may love Steven. Could he ever be mine?

Monday 15th September

No he couldn't. He's gone off with Andrew who I have to say is working his way through the staff on this ward like a dose of salts. I've told Veronica to watch out.

Mr Fodder-Chapman is going home today. It turns out his visitor was not his sister. That's one of the harder things about this job: you get attached to people and then they just leave. You never get to tell them to change their pyjamas again. He buys us all a box of chocolates and I think he gives me a special little wink as he leaves. I'm of an age when a girl should be thinking of marriage but unless you work in A and E, where all the policeman hang about, it's not easy to find a husband round here. I may have to start going down the fire station but surely things haven't quite come to that yet.

I have been thinking about this job again. Maybe the moral guardian thing is a bit of a red herring. It seems to me that I have to be like the E grades but more so, except when Sister Mercy isn't here, when I have to be like her but less so. I think that just about covers it.

Tuesday 16th September

Steven was very tearful today. When he wasn't throwing himself across the freshly made beds sobbing uncontrollably he was singing 'I Will Survive' at the top of his crackling voice. He said he had been cast off by Andrew like a discarded tissue. Sister Mercy says that Andrew is a psychopath. So on top of everything else the floozy can see into the future. I suggest to Steven that he comes round and we play old records and have a little cigarette.

We listen to 'It Should Have Been Me' about 35 times. We need chocolate and so we phone Sarah Burton-West. Andrew answers. We hang up. We phone Sister Mercy and she comes round with three boxes of mini Swiss rolls. We all worship at the altar of Sister Mercy.

Wednesday 17th September

The woman with short hair and the nosestud is dying. Her name is Clara. She is nice.

Mr Fodder-Chapman phones the ward and asks for me. He asks if I would like to go out.

'What about your lady friend?' I ask.

'She's living with someone,' he says. 'A psychiatric nurse called Andrew and they are going to go off together.'

'They probably need a rest,' I say.

'That's what they said,' he answers.

I agree to go out with Mr Fodder-Chapman but not before I make my speech about how he may have grown attached to me in my nursing role but I am also a woman with interests and that it is the woman with interests he would be taking out not the nurse. Not that I won't still be a nurse but I certainly won't be wearing my uniform or anything sordid like that. He says that he understands professional boundaries and that he just hopes that he will have the chance to get to know me.

Sister Mercy takes me for a drink. I find myself feeling tearful and wonder if this is unprofessional. It isn't like me. Clara is 26 and she has cancer. She has not had many visitors. Two, I think.

Friday 19th September

I have been an F grade for exactly five weeks now. I tell Mr Fodder-Chapman of my hopes and my dreams. He seems surprised.

'You are a nurse,' he says, 'isn't that enough? And by the way my leg hurts; what do you think that is?' I realise that Mr Fodder-Chapman is less than I may have hoped.

I tell Steven on the phone. He tells me I deserve better. I agree. I have decided that I shall do another course. I already have under my belt the following certificates: Nursing the Distressed Patient; The Sociology of Pain; Management for Beginners; The Role of Complementary Therapies in Nursing; and Portuguese for Beginners. All but the Portuguese were pointless. I have told Sister Mercy that I would like to take a course in Nursing the Dying Patient.

Monday 22nd September

Steven is in love which is nice. They met at a mosaic evening class. I did an evening class in mosaics once. The only person I got on with was a girl who worked as a secretary at the local paper. Good money they get down there.

Clara has a new visitor. A thin young man who is apparently her boyfriend. I don't like him; he should have come in before now. Clara seems pleased to see him. I think I saw him crying and she was comforting him. She has lovely eyes. After he goes I find five minutes for a quick chat. She is quite new to the area, she moved up here to be near the thin man.

'Was it worth it?' I ask.

'Oh yes,' she says. She doesn't have a job; she's been doing voluntary advice work in town. She doesn't have many friends here yet she said.

'Is there anything you want?' I ask.

'No,' she says.

Sister Mercy says she may not go on holiday just yet. She doesn't say why.

Thursday 25th September

Veronica Bake is upset. She is crying because of Clara. Veronica has not worked consistently with someone who is dying before.

Sarah Burton-West, who is half the woman she was, has met a nice man at Weight Watchers.

'Isn't he fat?' I ask.

'He's fatter than he will be,' she says, 'but I wouldn't call him fat.'

'Well of course you wouldn't, it's rude,' I say.

'No I mean he isn't actually all that fat.'

'Then why is he at Weight Watchers?'

'I think he likes fat women,' she said.

Sister Mercy says that she is no longer going out with Ali the charge nurse. She suggests we have a ward night out, just the girls. Steven said that would be smashing and everyone laughed. I didn't get it but I laughed as well. So at the weekend me and Sister Mercy and Veronica and Sarah and Steven and Rita the auxiliary and Rebecca (the quiet one who has worked on this ward since about 1942 and has spoken to me about twice since I've been here) are going into town and we are wearing our best clothes.

Sunday 28th September

Clara is going home, at least for a few days. Her boyfriend has come to pick her up.

'Nice of him to pop in,' I say to Sister Mercy.

'I know him,' she says.

'Where from, Visitors Anonymous?'

'His mother died in here three months ago. You nursed her Nancy, don't you remember? He came every day. I think he must hate it here.'

Last night we went out. Steven didn't stay long: his new man whisked him away to something fashionable. I must say Rebecca surprised me: she drank like a fish, smoked like a beagle and still didn't speak very much. Catherine told us about the first time her and her new boyfriend did it. She said it was very nice but his penis was a funny shape.

'What sort of funny shape?' said Sister Mercy.

'Triangular,' said Catherine.

Sister Mercy and Rebecca and Rita laughed and Veronica blushed but I just didn't get it. Surely going to bed with a man who has a penis with three points is a bad thing unless you are three of the admirably inseparable Nolan sisters. We went back to Sister Mercy's and smoked the last of Andrew's funny cigarettes. Rita said this was good stuff and baked a cake really really quickly. Sarah had five slices. Veronica asked her about the diet but she said that her new boyfriend, whose name was Colin, kept buying her chocolate so what the hell.

Tuesday 30th September

I wish I had a boyfriend. One of the medical students asked me out today but he hasn't started shaving yet – not properly anyway judging by the amount of toilet roll stuck to his face. He wants to be a surgeon.

Clara's thin boyfriend came in today to talk to Sister Mercy. He was here for about an hour. She wasn't actually on duty but what the hell. I bumped into him as he left and asked how Clara was. He said she was in pain and he hated seeing her in pain. He wanted to take her to London for a few days so she could see her friends but he was worried about pain control.

I have decided to reply to some lonely hearts adverts and I have persuaded Veronica to play too. She agreed at Sister Mercy's the other night. Mind you she also declared that she was a little space onion and she wanted some alien to peel her. Sister Mercy told her she needed sex. Veronica blushed. And that's when I asked her. We read through the local adverts yesterday. I wrote off to Handsome of Walsall and she replied to Shy from Wolverhampton. I think we are very brave.

Friday 3rd October

Mr Wince died today.

I got a reply from Handsome of Walsall. He sent me a photograph but unfortunately I don't think it was him. Sister Mercy said it was George Clooney and she was pretty sure that Mr Clooney (who is apparently a heart-throb pretend-doctor on the television as well as being Batman) doesn't live in Walsall. Veronica has not heard from Shy from Wolverhampton, which suggests to me that Shy from Wolverhampton is less of a liar than Handsome of Walsall.

Friday 10th October

It turns out that Handsome of Walsall is Andrew. I don't know where he finds the time. Sister Mercy says that he must be desperately insecure but I think he is mainly exhausted. Rita gives me a little present: it's a couple of rolled-up cigarettes. I wonder if I may be a drug addict. In my heart I am against all things sinful. But sometimes the days just seem to take over and run themselves and I find myself behaving in the strangest of ways. For example, on Tuesday I slept with a student. Looking on the bright side, he wasn't a student nurse; that would have been just too much to bear for my increasingly frail self-esteem. On the down side, he was a philosophy student so he has no money and no prospects. Nice man though.

Friday 17th October

I have been neglecting my diary of late but so much has been happening I'm all in a spin. They've appointed a clinical nurse specialist on an H grade. I am aghast, amazed, stunned. I would have thought that they would just have promoted Sister Mercy and I said this to her.

'I did not apply for the post,' she said.

'Why not?' I asked.

'I like it here,' she said.

'You're not just saying that, are you?' I said.

'No,' she said.

'It's not that you don't think we're any good without you, is it?'

'No,' she said.

I was relieved, but mainly I was glad that Sister Mercy was not going anywhere. We are getting a nice little team together here.

However my aghastness turned to absolute flabberaghastness when the new clinical nurse specialist walked in. It was the kidney stone girl and she had her own bloody whistle.

'You,' she said.

'Me?' I said.

'Yes,' she said.

'Hello ma'am,' I said, curtseying.

'You didn't treat me terribly well when I was here did you?'

'I wouldn't say that,' I said.

'You didn't ask me my name until the day before I left, you did not do a care plan and you were late with pain control. In fact, regardless of how much pain I was in, you did not come straight to me when I was due pethidine. You started at the other end of the ward.'

'We always start at the other end of the ward.'

'Why?' she said.

'It's routine,' I said.

'You are supposed to be an F grade nurse. What if Sister Mercy has a bungee-jumping accident one day and you are in charge? God help our patients.'

I began to cry.

'Stop snivelling, you stupid girl,' said the vegetarian, 'and remember, I've got my eye on you.'

Sister Mercy was very nice. She said that I had been neglectful but that it was a difficult time for me, being new to the post. She said I had been a pompous tight-arse with the insight of chipboard. The thing to do is to make sure that it isn't the normal way of things. She asked me if I was upset about anything at the time.

I said, 'No, I just wasn't thinking.'

She smiled and said, 'So think.'

Monday 20th October

We got a postcard from Clara and her boyfriend. They said they were having a great time.

I think Veronica is sleeping with Shy from Wolverhampton but she hasn't seen him naked yet. She says this suits her just fine as the triangular penis story rather upset her.

I think I need a holiday. I want to know what has happened to me. I never used to be so self-conscious and judgmental. I went to a pop festival last year for chrissakes! I may have let my lofty position go to my head there for a while. I'm an F grade. This is a position of responsibility. I'm almost a senior member of staff. Sister Mercy let me blow her whistle the other day. She says that she and I are not allowed to travel on the same bus any more in case there is an accident. But it may be that I got a little carried away. You see that? That's reflection, that is, self-learning. I must remember to photocopy my diary and put it in my PREP portfolio.

The philosophy student called round. He has absolutely no bloody money but at least he doesn't ask me for mine. My mum thought I was going to marry a doctor but Sister Mercy says you should never sleep with someone who knows that much about your body before you've even taken your clothes off. The philosophy student wants me to go to Greece with him.

'How will we afford it?' I asked.

'I've got somewhere to stay,' he said. 'Some friends have a villa so we just need our flights and our spending money.'

The vegetarian Marxist kidney stone woman glares at me every time she sees me, so maybe a holiday would be a good thing.

Sarah Burton-West is the size of a yacht again. Veronica gets a call from Shy from Wolverhampton every day at work and they whisper things like 'You're snuggly buggly' into the phone to each other. It won't last. Nothing does. But while it's not lasting, it's good to make the most of it.

THE 'G' GRADE

◆ ◆ ◆ ◆ ◆ ◆ ◆

MOVING SWIFTLY ON TO GIN THERAPY....
•Aromatherapy
•Homeopathy
• Psycho-therapy
etc etc

This is the equivalent of a black belt. The lowest-paid expert in the country, yet it should be the best-paid job in nursing. It does us no harm to remember the old adage 'Those who can, do, those who can't, teach and those who can't teach take up research positions or go into journalism.'

For all the investigations and research that go on in nursing these days, all the evidence-based practice pursuits and all the pretend intelligence that is exercised 'thinking' about nursing, nobody really asks the hard questions. Like: how do good nurses sustain good practice over a long period of time? And this question leads to another: how do we hold on to our best and most experienced clinicians?

The current method, chosen by experts, is the sado-masochistic approach, as borne out by the Code of Conduct. The central theme of the Code is not appropriately referenced, but harks back to some of the early works of the Marquis de Sade. You, the nurse, are personally responsible 24 hours a day for the public perception and confidence invested in nursing. You will never do anything that in any way offends that esteem. You will not swear in public, nor drink too much. If you are threatened you will turn the other cheek; if you are abused you will rise above it. When out dancing, if people for any reason know that you are a nurse you will dance in a controlled fashion, and will not, under any circumstances, throw your arms around. Apart from the indignity that this brings to the profession, you may have someone's eye out and you of all people should know that health promotion in discos is important. It's no good you thinking that the austerity of nursing as presented by these people actually colludes with the 'quiet angelic girl' image that many think has prevented any political progress for nurses since about 1432. If you are a nurse you have to be morally superior.

The chances are, however, that the UKCC have been staying round at the ENB's house in the local village where it is still 1934. A public image of nursing doesn't really exist anymore. Media images run from the modern Spice Girl type of nurse to the Barbara

Windsor type of nurse. From the nursery nurse who shelters children from a machete attack with her body to nurses convicted of serious crimes. Overwhelmingly, however, the public all have a personal contact with nurses and that is where they gather their opinions. They have either been nursed or know a nurse or know someone who has been nursed. And they come away and say that the nurses were good or the nursing was crap or they were rushed off their feet or I didn't see a nurse the whole time I was there. They do not say, 'It's terrible, my nurse was very good but I suspect she has the Prodigy album and may drink beer.' The only people who want nurses to behave like Doris Day did in 1953 are the ones who read the Daily Express and they don't realise that actually the Daily Express is meant to be ironic. These people don't just want nurses to be quiet gals from the back of the class, to be useful and obedient until it's time for them to breed. They want all gals to be like that and they want all men to be like William Hague. I really don't think we should encourage such shenanigans.

Nurses do not have a responsibility to be better or worse or different from anybody else. When they are at work they have the responsibility to do their jobs well. If a nurse is convicted of rape or murder then of course they should never work again. But if a nurse gets drunk or has an argument in the street or shouts loudly at a football match, so what?

The only other professions where people are expected to behave perfectly and professionally (I really don't know what that means outside of a clinical context) at all times are policemen and nuns. Policemen are only expected not to break the law, beyond that their professional body doesn't care, and as for nuns, well, things are just different for nuns. I don't get nuns; one minute they're not allowed to speak for 20 years and have to live in a hut with other nuns thinking about stuff, and the next they are making films with Whoopi Goldberg, singing their little nun heads off, or wandering around Austria climbing every mountain. The model of a modern profession presented by nunning is not, I believe, the way forward for nursing.

So what's it going to take to keep you doing what you do? Money? Money and a more conducive nursing environment? Whilst you are waiting, how are you going to sustain yourself? Emotionally, holistically, clinically. I didn't; I needed a break. Others don't either; they leave and go into organisational psychology or become air stewards.

Now that you are a G grade, I'm curious. When you are not surveying all you care for and working and planning and managing and knowing – what do you think of nursing now? Does it feel like a vocation to you? Do you feel like an angel? When you see the crass admiring references made to the angelic nature of the nurse do you smile inside, proud and reassured by the respect you are being afforded? Or do you want to throw up, preferably on the shirt of the patronising git who is respecting you, loving the thought of you, maybe even fantasising about you? Do you ever want to stuff the angel word down the throat of the smug man who, by liking you and what you do, is showing he cares? Caring vicariously is, after all, quicker than being useful and somehow more manly.

Are you tired? Do you have any regrets? Do you look at the people coming into nursing now and wonder who they are, why they are? Or do they fill you with inspiration? Do you read, occasionally, of the things that are happening in your profession and feel bemused? Do you wonder why your leaders are so blind and unknowing or do you admire them for their dedication and experience, smarting for them when they are unfairly criticised?

If you were told tomorrow that the Prime Minister was coming to your ward, or the Queen or someone, would you feel honoured and move the patients around so the healthiest ones are nearest their line of vision? Would you allow your ward to be decorated and re-carpeted for the important guests or demand the money be invested in a new staff nurse? Would you boast of the wonders of the hospital to your important visitors, or complain about the difficulties? The chances are you would be placed under enormous pressure to curtsey and be treated like an angel.

The last thing I was before I became what I am now, was a G

grade. I'd been an H grade but was crap at it and hated it anyway. So I went back to E and eventually found my way, more by accident than intent, to G. It's true what they say: 'Life is like a game of snakes and ladders', although increasingly it feels like a game of Mousetrap. As I recall (and it wasn't that long ago) the thing that concerned me most was safety. My unit was a self-referral walk-in service for those patients who had severe and enduring mental health problems but were difficult to engage. They could come in crisis, or for support, or for a coffee and a chat, or just to get out of the bedsits they tended to live in. We were never staffed properly and on many occasions things happened that potentially threatened the safety of staff or the patients. I found myself feeling responsible for that safety and caught between the trite ongoing arguments with cash-strapped managers for more staff and keeping the service available to the hundreds of patients who used it. I don't imagine for one moment that that is even close to being unusual.

So that's pay and responsibility. How many of you actually feel you have a voice? Let's be honest: there is a world peripheral to the practice of nursing. It exists in the magazines and the journals, in the organisations and the ambits of administrators. All have commentators and spokespeople, few of whom are actually still in practice (and how much time do you have to commentate on, reflect publicly, write about or generally politic about the experience?). Every G grade nurse I have ever known (and I admit that most of them are in mental health) really could not give a damn about fighting the good fight at the end of their working day. To be perfectly honest, I don't think I trust people who do. I suspect that at best the boundaries between themselves and their work are blurred and at worst they are obsessed or self-serving individuals who need to get out more. Of course I could be wrong and a little warped; maybe they are those perennial angels.

Even locally, how much power – real power, I mean – do you have to develop or plan services? None or little? So that's no money, lots of responsibility and little power. The simplest recipe for stress is responsibility without power. Of course most of you find a way of easing any overwhelming disparity that exists there, but that easing in itself takes a lot of thought, and perhaps a lot of effort.

Most of you find ways of sustaining yourself in the face of this, admittedly simple, scenario. A lot of you probably couldn't explain in detail how you do it. You find yourself using skills that are sophisticated and maybe difficult to pass on. A few of you, I suspect (and utter these words quietly) are close to burnout. I have worked with nurses who have been around at about charge nurse level for upwards of 15 years. They nurse like a spitting cat – they have forgotten why they do it. In a crisis they go one of two ways. Either they back away, gun-shy or afraid, and hide in the toilet while the resuscitation team does its work. Or they wake up, spring into life and nurse like gods.

The vast majority of you, of course, just do your job, the way people always do their job no matter what it is. I'll come back to the majority. For others, the whole thing has left its scars and there appears to be something of a moratorium on speaking about them. There are the nurses who work in HIV but don't practice safe sex; nurses who work in drink and drug services and who drink and drug; and numbers of nurses who have addiction problems, and the many others who are so used to the extreme circumstances that surround them daily that they replicate emotional and social extremes in their own lives because anything less leaves them unmoved. Most of these behaviours are not chosen, nor even considered; they just are. Whilst there is no such thing as a typical nurse, and whilst most nurses lead normal and contained lives, there are plenty who howl at the moon and turn their experiences and their feelings in on themselves.

It is said that if there are damaged people who nurse, it is down to who they were before they trained; that it was their desire to experience the extremes of life at first hand that drove them into front-line care in the first place. Maybe so, but the fact remains: nursing can damage your health.

A shade maudlin all this; perhaps I lack perspective. So I shall borrow from the retirement speech of Josie Flounder, a sister of 20 years. She said farewell recently and offered a kindly reflection on her experiences to those who gathered to say goodbye. Josie is double trained and has worked pretty much across the clinical board, and though she nursed like an angel she could reflect like a spitting cat.

'Friends, colleagues, nurses, pass me the sherry.

'I have heard it said that we nurses are less than what we were. And I have heard others suggest that we are more. Perhaps the pursuit of status and professionalisation has ripped us from our context. Perhaps it has even de-skilled us. On the other hand, maybe it has secured us at the core of care teams in all areas. Whatever, sometimes there are things that need to be said. I know that some of you are from a new breed. Raised in a climate of austerity which demands that professionalism extends beyond the way you treat your patients to the way you do your ironing, how you speak of the world and what you do with your boyfriend on your day off.

'Well I am part of a dying breed. Have you seen that film The Last of the Mohicans? I'm a bit like him. Obviously I'm not as fast a runner or anything, and I certainly slay fewer deer but in essence I am a bit of a beautiful relic. Perhaps I should just lay down and say nothing but where's the fun in that? Anyway I'm a bit bloody-minded. To stay at G grade for any length of time you have to be a bit bloody-minded.

'I have seen many things from you, my colleagues, and have on occasion been bemused by the many clinical and cultural changes that have surrounded me. Take for example some of the new professions. Now it may be that complementary therapists are a considered response to the promotional bottleneck that exists for you young things. You tend to branch outward when upward is not possible. It may be a wholehearted cultural response to the medico-scientific world that feels limiting in the context of how nursing feels to so many people. Or it may be an attempt by nurses to invest in genuinely independent practice. There are many valid reasons for the existence of alternative approaches to health care, and many valid reasons why nurses themselves may pursue some of these alternatives. But none of them quite excuses some of the funny bunnies – the whole, limited genre of 'otherness' that has been created.

'Fetch more sherry, I'm going to talk about the therapists.

'Take, for example, the art therapist. Hippies all of them. You can usually tell an AT by the fact that she is wearing a tie-dyed skirt. She may have had her colours done, so the chances are she looks like a melted traffic light in tan tights. She will talk more slowly than anyone else. At first you will think that this is because she must be choosing her words carefully, precisely. She isn't; she just thinks in colours. In fact she is looking at all the colours swaying around the room above your head. She is calm unless you hide her crayons, in which case she becomes a right little tiger. She doesn't remotely understand the culture of health care. But ask her to draw an orange and she'll think you mean it. She will take herself more seriously than anybody with an 'O' level in art has any right to.

'Art therapists say things like, "Ronnie did a wonderful picture today depicting the dark inner psyche that has brutally ripped his sense of reality from him. He has entered a realm, probably designed by his sense of detachment from his surroundings and it's going to take a lot of sensitive and considered interpretation to draw him back to us." And you will look at Ronnie's picture and say, "Yes but it's a cat isn't it? It's a cat, sat on the mat." And she'll say, "Yes it's a cat, but the cat represents Ronnie and the mat is his world. Ronnie is sitting on his world, he's trying to contain his world, to stop it from cascading outward." You will say to Ronnie, "Ronnie, what's the picture mate?" and he'll go, "That'll be a cat, you prat, and it's sat on the mat." "Is it a metaphor Ronnie?" And he'll say, "No its a tabby," You and Ronnie will laugh and the art therapist will go home and she will take her cat with her.

'And then there is the music therapist.

'As above but louder. Never, ever, ever get stuck in lift with two music therapists. Within three minutes you'll be 'Kumbayah-ing my lord' like a Salvation Army sergeant. Half an hour later they will have dismantled the emergency telephone in order to construct some kind of percussion instrument and you will be the fool banging away on the damn thing in perfect time to 'London's Burning'. You will keep missing your cue on the third harmony vocal, and they'll just smile those really smug 'I started piano lessons before I was born' smiles and show you EXACTLY where to come in the next time. And I'll tell you this: none of them can sing for toffee, but does that stop them shrieking away like Dame Tiki Whatshername? Does it hell.

'Having said that, the music therapists do have a vital role to play in most well-staffed health care settings: they talk to the art therapists. And great conversations they are too.

"What's your favourite colour?"

"Yellow. What's your favourite noise?"

'Leave them to it. About once every three months they will approach the core team and say that they have had an idea. Chances are they will be lying.

'Yes, yes I know they have their uses, but so do pop socks and we don't try to make them an integral part of the multi-disciplinary team.

'And then there's all these complementary therapies. I think it's safe to say I've had a go at most of them. I've had to. Increasingly over the years my nurses have trained in one 'opathy' or another. I rather enjoyed some of them – acupuncture is smashing and homeopathy cleared up my sinuses a treat – but they are a pleasant-smelling side-show. There are more complementary therapists in this country than there are GPs. Complementary therapies are the health care equivalent of comfort food. In mental health they are nice because they feel nice: the contact is reassuring; the 'science' is less invasive; and the responsibility is taken from the patient just as much as it is with the worst excesses of medicine. It's been said before and I'll say it again: I'll consider complementary therapies truly alternative when places with medical crises call for aromatherapists to help rather than doctors and nurses.

'The beauty and reason for the proliferation of complementary therapies are of course obvious: they are humane. The contact is gentle, the curiosity of a homeopathic assessment humanises the patient's experience the way a nurse's touch or smile did 30 years ago and the way systematic problem-orientated nursing doesn't. The way of the alternative therapists – a softness, an interest in the being of the patient – is the way nursing almost went when it emerged from the gender-driven nonsense of the 1960s and before, but it got too embarrassed and instead turned to science. Don't get me wrong; I don't mind. I don't hark back to the days of bed-baths and doctors' handmaidens. I just hoped the so-called revolution would have brought more.

'As for our colleagues in the other professions – and I must say its nice to see so many of you here – I do wish you physiotherapists would stop doing press-ups in the corner and you OTs would stop throwing that bloody sponge ball at the doctors. But in the main, I'm glad you came. Apparently you take us more seriously now. I'm not convinced, you can be terribly pompous sometimes, especially you social workers. I know it's part of the job description but so is helping patients fill in Disability Living Allowance forms, and you are not quite so zealous in the pursuit of that are you?

'I like inter-profession mocking. It is the only funny way that we feel sorry for ourselves, and so long as it doesn't get out of hand (as it did with the social workers versus nurses hockey match last year) I rather enjoy it. In fact I think the reality is, we have more and more in common. We all feel undervalued, unheard, underpaid and overworked. We all feel that what we do is significant and important and we are all right.

'Within nursing itself, and here I speak from experience, there appears to be a massive cultural clash haunting nursing at the moment. A clash, if you will, between those who premise their practice on the apprenticeship models of learning from the past, and with it the implicit starting point of patient contact, and those who premise their routine on university learning and the starting point of theory before activity, a process of reflective and considered practice. As the new ones come into nursing, the conflict manifests itself in lots of different ways and, to be frank, we have not always dealt with it as well as we might. I for one have had to put a stop to the weekly five-a-side football matches between the 'old guard' and the 'new broom' teams. The stud-marks left on junior staff nurse Betty Persil's left thigh were no accident.

'I wonder if eventually things will only resolve themselves when all the nurses who trained the old way (it was only 10 years ago for Christ's sake) actually retire in about 2025. Perhaps we should remember the old pop adage, 'What we need is a great big melting pot', a large kettle essentially, which we all have to get into and allow our differences to merge into one. There are those of course who think that differences should not be eliminated; indeed they should be celebrated. In the main I would agree but frankly, and I say this with some sadness, nursing does not appear to be mature or intelligent enough to enjoy the differences it breeds. Mind you, saying that, I personally would not get into a kettle with any doctors; I draw the line there. I don't want to merge with a doctor, no not even you George Clooney; well not in a kettle anyway.

'Some people say I have some strange ways. Why, for example do I insist that all handovers be conducted in the style of a West End musical? Team-building, that's why; that and the fact that I love to see staff nurse Robert de Crumb and Betty Persil reciting the mornings news to the incoming staff to the tune of 'You're the one that I want'. Ridiculous, you say? Maybe so, but nobody is ever late for my handovers. However I feel I have a few things to pass on to the newer members of staff, so I will.

'Always be prepared to take on the most difficult, challenging or complex situation that is presented to your service. The rest of your staff will be reassured by this and it is your responsibility to reassure both clinically and professionally. It is also the case that you are probably the most qualified person to do this because, despite what you may be told to the contrary, being a G grade is essentially a clinical position.

'Be prepared to delegate. I used to get this wrong a lot of the time I'm afraid. I would confuse looking after my staff with managing them effectively. It took me a while to sort this out. I realised I was doing it wrong when my F grade came to me and said she felt undervalued and I put her in charge of watching out for any abuse in the distribution of biscuits amongst the staff. She said that whilst she was pleased to see that I was able to trust her with something which up to then had required the use of surveillance cameras, she felt capable of more. I admit that when I got bronchial pneumonia in 1995 and had to take three days off sick, you could have knocked me down with a feather when I returned to find the unit had not missed me. I was rather hurt to be honest. What am I if I'm not indispensable? Have I worked all these years only for people to go and manage without me when my lungs go a bit wonky for a couple of days?

'Fetch me gin, I'm feeling sorry for myself.

'Know that you will, on occasion, find yourself managing nurses who are either crap, lazy, stupid or permanently confused. I know we are not supposed to admit this but everyone knows it's true. I admit that I have in my time hated the nurse who is rubbish more than I have hated Hattie, the hated, despot dictator from evil valley. One can't help but expect good nursing from nurses and so the sense of disappointment in the face of a bad one is somehow all the harder to swallow. For example, I got myself a newly qualified Keith on the ward a few years ago and he asked for long-term study leave before he asked where the fire exits were. He spoke to me about career development more than he spoke to the patients about anything. He was always late, didn't know where we kept little things like sheets and the drug trolley, and never asked questions, especially of women, because questions were beneath him.

'One of my colleagues once sent him down to A and E to pick up a new admission called Eileen Dover and he didn't get it even after he'd wandered around casualty for about a month asking "Have you seen Eileen Dover?" and everyone had laughed at him. I am ashamed to say I got rid of him the coward's way: I gave him a reference. He's something irritating in the community now. I would not do that again but of course it's difficult to get rid of crap staff. For all the talk of regulation and standards, in the main they don't work. If you get yourself a Keith, manage him closely, help him to nurse, and make his choices clear to him: either he nurses well or at least adequately, or you give him a big Chinese burn or he has to leave. For all the anxieties about staff retention, there is a big difference between losing a valued, skilled, committed but slightly broken or tired nurse and losing a Keith. Not just anyone can nurse, you know.

'Know more clearly than you know anything else where your professional boundaries are: all of them – as a professional, a helper, a manager, a confidant and a clinician. Without this knowledge becoming etched on your soul, you will not be able to function.

'When managers come to you with a proposal, never say yes until you are perfectly clear about what the long-term consequences are and you have discussed them openly. It may be that your manager comes to you and says, "We are going to buy your day hospital a small coach for day trips, or rather a drug company is going to buy it for you. However you will be able to transport elderly patients to and from the hospital and have the occasional outing." And you think, "Smashing, at last a proposal that can't backfire and can only benefit." And then you find out that the coach was built in 1856 and requires four horses, which you have to buy by running tombolas and jumble sales every week for the next three years. And you have to take the horses home and keep them in your third-floor flat, and your husband is allergic to horses. Should this ever happen to you by the way, I advise you to run the tombolas to the best of your ability, buy the horses and then free the horses. Don't tell me that there is no place for free horses in inner-city areas. Nature will find a way, so just free the horses.

'OK the bar is open. I have probably painted a less than beautiful picture but I would say this. I would have done nothing other than this given the choice. If God said to me, "Josie, you can go round again and this time you can be anything you please; do you want to be an astronaut? A film star, a millionairess? Anything." I would look God squarely in the eye and say, "I would like to be an astronaut for a week, a film star for a day and a millionairess when

I retire but I'll do the nurse thing again please." And I imagine that God would fill up a little and smile, and we would embrace but not kiss because God doesn't kiss, not with tongues anyway. Let's hit the bar.'

Josie's is just one of a hundred stories out there. There are of course plenty of nurses who have left and there are plenty more who vaguely consider leaving over a long period of time. Some of them train at evening class to be accountants or herbalists; others vaguely plan to start vegetarian restaurants on Greek islands. And, despite protestations to the contrary, there are some weird ones too.

For example, in the early 1980s there was a charge nurse working on a psychiatric rehabilitation ward that perhaps did less rehabilitation than it might. Each day he would write in the notes. 'No change today' (used to happen, honest). He decided that this was not really good enough. But perhaps missed the point. Rather than doing anything with the patient that would cause something to change, he felt the problem was one of writing style. And so he swore never again to write 'No change today'. He began with 'No alteration in patient's behaviour' and moved on to 'The ongoing life force of said client has remained constant', 'The developmental route is unblemished by variation', and finally 'In this ever-changing world in which we live, where nature is eternally adapting to new possibilities and the human condition forces us to strive for bigger, better, faster and greater, where technology and history combine to speed up life and the universe, the patient has chosen, it seems, to ignore this tirade of activity that spins relentlessly around his head and went to bed early.'

I said at the beginning that nursing is the new rock and roll. Well in the rock and roll circus that is health service life, the G grade is Elvis Presley and the Beatles rolled into one. That is not to say that the G grade nurse eats too much peanut butter and insists on wearing tasselled tops that really don't fit. I mean that the G grade is the king of rock and roll.

It is of course just a matter of time before Hollywood realises this and starts making action adventure films with Bruce Willis or

Demi Moore or Nicole Kidman playing action-hero nurses. We are half-way there with ER and all those programmes where the nurses and doctors are the heroes, but there just aren't enough car chases.

I understand that early next year there is to be a major Hollywood blockbuster based around the exploits of a community mental health team. It will star Demi and Bruce, with Steven Segal as the all-kicking all-punching family therapist, Michelle Pfeiffer as the former Olympic gymnast turned community team leader who has a patient with an obsessive compulsive disorder to blow up the world. He will be played, of course, by Steve Buscemi or John Malkovich. The plot has it that Steve or John is a nice person who can't help himself and steals some nuclear bombs, when he really should be in a problem-solving group run by Bruce. Bruce, calling on his nursing experience, feeds back at the team meeting, and Michelle remembers that Steve or John told her that he knew where the US Government keeps spare bombs and had the code to the bicycle lock that constituted security.

The CIA get involved and want to kill Steve or John but the community mental health team are against this idea. The CIA try anyway but bungle their attempt. Instead they shoot Sylvester Stallone, who didn't even know he was in the film. The Community Mental Health Team are called upon in America's darkest hour to seek out and offer twice-weekly sessions to Steve or John, without the aid of the safety net of a community detention order and armed only with their travel cards and their wits. Demi soon steals a car which means the local police, led by Robert De Niro, are after the CMHT. It really is a battle against time.

Some of the stunts are brilliant. In a tense climax Steven Segal offers cognitive behavioural therapy on top of a speeding train loaded with high explosives. Unfortunately he offers it to the wrong person, as Steve or John is actually on top of the Empire State Building with his bomb cleverly disguised as a large sandwich. Whilst Steven cures the train driver of his fear of trains, which is a touching sub-plot, Bruce and Demi and Michelle arrive just in time before Steve or John detonates the sandwich. They arrange themselves and a few celebrity passers-by (including Quentin Tarantino and Eddie Murphy in a hilarious cameo) into a circle and conduct a climactic group session where Steve or John (probably Steve actually) discloses the history of his obsessive behaviour from the point where he used to polish his bathroom taps 13 times a day to where he stole nuclear weapons, even though deep down he didn't want to.

As is the way of Hollywood films they have filmed two endings. In one, Bruce looks like he dies by diving on Steve's sandwich and saving New York, but miraculously he survives and marries Steve's sister. Steve's sister is played by Minnie Driver, who decides to forego her promising career as a nuclear physicist to become a nurse. In the other ending, Demi shoots Michelle because it turns out that she was using hypnotherapy to control Steve's obsessions in a warped attempt to make the city of New York pay members of community mental health teams appropriate travel expenses. Michelle is merely winged and, calling upon her gymnastic skills, she cartwheels into Demi, sits on her and does some solution-focused therapy whilst Bruce fetches help.

The film closes with the team meeting the following morning, where they reflect on a patient with a psychotic depression who is planning to strap himself to the Space Shuttle. The team are welcoming aboard a new member, who will be played by John Cusack. 'Oh no,' says Michelle, smiling at Demi who is feeling better since her session with Michelle on the Empire State Building, 'here we go again.' John says, 'Is this normal for you guys?' Everyone laughs and Bruce says, 'Hey, you're a nurse now.'

Could happen.

The Academic

◆ ◆ ◆ ◆ ◆ ◆ ◆

This broad-based term covers a multitude of sins. You may be a teacher; you may be a researcher; you may be an author offering up a cleverly considered analysis of nursing or health care. You may be a professor or a research assistant. The days when academics wore mortar boards and long black capes whilst holidaying in Provence are long gone. Academics are, thankfully, no longer dusty old men who believe jazz music marked the demise of civilisation. These days anybody can be vaguely academic. Of course, money helps and, despite our liberated times, child care and financial support for the most needy and talented individuals make education and research near-impossible for many. I hope you are not put off. Teaching and researching in the broadest sense is increasingly the obvious career choice for talented but clinically tired individuals. It does seem, however, just a tad too masculine at present, don't you think?

Of course, fundamentally, the relationship that exists between nursing and the universities is an economic one. The universities have to generate funds independently of government investment now, so they sell their services pretty much like health trusts. They sell places and services to nursing. However, universities have to be actively involved in research so they also have to apply for funding. When they have done their research, the research needs to be published and for this they get rating points which supposedly serve to measure their effectiveness. (Not that the universities understand the concept of clinical effectiveness, bless them.) However, the points are not based on social worth, nor even on the ability to disseminate the findings or ideas that the research comes up with. They are awarded according to the austerity of the journal in which they appear. Top marks are awarded for publication in journals which sell about eight copies a month to other people whose ambition extends no further than one day getting their own dreadfully written nonsense published in the same journals. I for one can certainly see that the world is going to become a better place as a result.

A word of advice, if I may: don't take yourself too seriously when you get a job in a university. You are going to find yourself surrounded by earnest social scientists measuring bits of life with all the zeal of a tabloid journalist trapped in Frank Bough's bedroom. Restrain yourself. I know it's going to be difficult; there is a creeping pressure to demonstrate your intellectual vigour at every opportunity, to prove yourself worthy of the title academic. Do not succumb to it. Here is why:

Firstly, the best academics – the most impressive, intelligent and convincing – are the ones who look like they are not trying. They are the ones secure enough to carry on wondering when lesser minds are reaching for often trite conclusions, additional qualifications and crass research ratings points.

Secondly, nobody likes a self-important sociologist. Absolutely nobody. The boyfriends of self-important sociologists are all having affairs. The parents of self-important sociologists all live abroad or at the very least change their names and never open the door to strangers. Some of them have taken up the opportunity afforded them by a sympathetic government to assume totally new identities. Most of them lie about the occupations of their children. When asked, 'So what is little Tina doing now; still nursing?' they say, 'No she had to stop doing that. She is a burglar now.' Remember, sociology is philosophy for the impatient.

Thirdly, you will lose all sense of perspective. Remember the beginning of your career? All those ideas about doing good and helping people? There is not the remotest hope of doing that if you take yourself and your silly search for truths too seriously. Every week you are an academic, ask yourself a question that is not easy to answer. Remind yourself of the only truth that history has left us with: the laughable fallibility of human knowledge. Try questions like, 'If a picture paints a thousand words, then why can't I paint you?' If it's good enough for Telly Savalas, it's good enough for you. Or, 'If I could talk to the animals what would I say to the chicken? Would I apologise for the whole breast or leg phenomenon? Or would I go on the offensive and say, "So you are allegedly a bird and yet you can't fly for toffee; explain yourself chicken!"'

OK, now, students. Don't be smug towards the students. It's hard enough taking in all the experiences, skill development, knowledge and hostility they are likely to face without some intellectually inadequate senior lecturer telling them that the only experiences worth reflecting on are the quantifiable ones and the route to good nursing is good essay writing. Stop it now, you're just showing off, and the rest of us will hate you and not invite you to the good parties or say nice things about you. In fact, we will openly mock your taste in music regardless of how informed we may be. We will spread rumours to the effect that you like Chris De Burgh and that you pretend you are a Spice Girl when your wife is out and practice all the dance moves and all that 'zigga zig aah' nonsense in front of the mirror, and we know because the neighbours told us.

Having got that off my chest, it's not all bad. If you are focused about what it is you want to do, you might just help change the world. Just be clear about two things. Why are you asking the questions you are asking, and what might be the consequences of your labours? If the answers are things like, 'The professor next door will be impressed and I may get a bigger office,' I'd let it go. Don't be impressed by professors. There are, and this is a sociological fact, as many professors of nursing as there are E grade staff nurse vacancies in the British Isles. Which points to a little mentioned solution to the staffing crisis.

The fundamental triumph of form over content is manifested by many of the thousands of bits of health-based research carried out every year. When you ask the researchers who are interested in discovering 'whether or not working recurrent night shifts affects sleep patterns' exactly why they chose that subject, they may say that they were genuinely interested in the outcome. Or they may say that they were practising their grasp of research methodology. As for the question itself, might not your average household cleaning implement have been able to take a wild guess at the findings? It's been about three years since I worked nights so I may be out of touch, but I distinctly remember that one of the rules was that you weren't allowed to go home to bed at 11pm, even if you pointed out to your patients that 11pm was your bed time on a school night. Furthermore you were not allowed to take your bed to work with you, attend the handover from the day shift in night attire or have a few friends round for a pyjama party.

In a vaguely liberal attempt to be fair, I must say that some researchers seem very committed, thoughtful, experienced and clever. I honestly didn't know there was such a thing as a professor of nursing until I left practice and went to work with Nursing Times. I thought the esteem in which they tended to be held by non-clinicians was quite comical. But I get time to listen to some of them speak now and I read some of what they write, and some of it is very insightful and occasionally combative. Some of it, however, is laughable rubbish and nobody should ever feel unable to say that. We all have a stake in nursing and increasingly the voice of nursing exists away from practice. So if we come across nonsense it's important that we point and laugh lest they get away with being silly AND well paid.

I went to a lecture a few months ago given by an associate professor. He spent about three and a half days restating the obvious until people were fainting through overexposure to obviousness. Some of us formed an escape committee at the back, and finally tunnelled our way out. Unfortunately it was too late for the others. They were forced to buy his book and make approving noises before being released back into the community for counselling and normalisation.

Apparently he received his associate professorship – sponsored by a drugs company I understand – for reading a book that didn't have all that many pictures in it. What made the task so impressive was that the pictures that the book did contain did not immediately relate to the words on the opposite pages. So, for example, near the picture of a cat was a word other than 'cat'. It may have been 'mat' or 'sat' or something. So impressed were the people who gave out titles that they gave him one there and then. There is, of course, a fixation with titles in nursing at the moment. I suspect it's got something to do with status: a fancy job title is very useful at parties.

'So what do you do?'

'I'm a researcher in the sociology of nursing.'

'Oh that's nice, I knew a nurse once.'

'Yes I'm sure but I'm not a nurse. I'm more a sociologist.'

'Lovely girl, very good at rounders too ...'

'Yes but I'm a sociologist, an academic if you will.'

'Ooh she could whack a rounders ball. You wouldn't know it to look at her, slip of a thing. You wouldn't pick her first if, say, God told you to pick a rounders team to play against Satan's rounders team and if you lose the whole world would be sentenced to eternal damnation. But you'd be wrong; great rounders player. I often wonder what happened to her.'

'I'm not just a nurse, I do research, I've got a degree and it's not in nursing.'

'I think she may still be nursing. Of course she may have given it all up for rounders, you never know do you.'

'In fact I'd say a lot of research extends beyond nursing ...'

'I wonder if she was good at other sports or if it was just rounders ...'

'Listen, you don't understand. I'm not JUST a nurse. I don't play rounders, I do research, statistical and planned, into nursing.'

'Oh, you're not a proper nurse then?'

'No.'

'What do you do then?'

'I research things.'

'Like what?'

'Nursing ...'

'What's that about then?'

'Well some people nurse and others do research into nursing. How to nurse well, new ways of nursing, things like that.'

'Why?'

'Because that is the way we get better.'

'But you don't actually nurse ...'

'No.'

'And you don't play rounders?'

'No.'

'And you get paid for what do you?'

'Yes I get paid. I'm very well qualified and I'm knowledgeable.'

'What's the capital of Bhutan?'

'I don't know.'

'Who won the world cup in 1958?'

'What?'

'What was Kant's categorical imperative?'

'Was it a mail-order shopping company?'

'No, you're thinking of Kant's Catalogue Empire.'

'I'm guessing.'

'You're a sociologist, aren't you?'

'Yes, yes I am.'

'Do you know where your parents live?'

'No, no I don't.'

'And your girlfriend, she's sleeping with someone else isn't she?'

'Yes, yes she is.'

Of course it's easy to mock nursing academics but that shouldn't stop you doing it. There are few perks to nursing these days so the right to have a bit of a laugh in the face of the ridiculous becomes all the more important. However, now you are an academic you do have, in theory, an important job to do. It is your job to think about nursing, to make the practice and activity of nursing better. To give analysis and voice to the development of practice and profession. It is your job to think – creatively, systematically, responsibly – about the activity you know so well and love so much. Go on then, but remember the rest of us will only take you seriously if we think you know what you are talking about.

Ultimately the relationship between academia and nursing suffers a self-conscious credibility gap. Nursing is not historically a realm commonly associated with academia and one can't help but wonder if some people who work in academia are just a mite conscious of that. Good nursing has always required intelligence. But that clarity and flexibility of thought has never before needed to be institutionalised, which is essentially all that taking nursing into the universities has done. And unfortunately, waiting for nursing in the universities are some right bloody idiots.

Let's be honest: we all know some really good nurse educators. We all know of some really impressive researchers or thinkers committed to higher standards in practice and education and promoting nursing as an activity. But it's the rest of the bastards I can't stand.

Barbarella has a sister. Her name is Thelma and she has been a nurse for over 20 years, starting off as an EN before converting to RMN. I've worked with her in the past and she is a very good nurse – conscientious, with a very broad skills base. In her time Thelma has taken more courses than Christopher Columbus. Apparently if you take a lot of accredited courses you collect something called CATS points and they all add up until eventually you get either a nursing degree or a really nice toaster. Recently she was seconded onto the CPN course which, on completion, would give her a degree.

Thelma happens to be one of those people who is mildly intimidated by the thought of academia, imagining for some absurd reason that it may be beyond her. However, despite her misplaced concerns she enjoyed studying and worked very hard. At the end of her course she was awarded a first-class honours degree and was told that she had been given the highest marks ever awarded by her faculty.

She was understandably very proud and was asked to come in to see her nurse tutors. That's nurse tutors, OK? Whereupon Thelma was told that the tutors were so impressed with her work that they wanted to recommend that she give up nursing and do something more worthy of her talents. Like what? Chemical engineering? Geography? Or research perhaps.

And you wonder why these people are held in such low esteem? On the one hand university-based education is supposedly established as a process to support the knowledge base and credibility of nursing. Yet, when it is successfully negotiated, the mere act of nursing well is considered lowly, far beneath such high minds.

I'm told by the way that one does not refer to teachers as tutors any more. Ten years ago they were tutors, then they became teachers, then lecturers, then educationists, then educationalists. That constitutes seven new letters in less than a decade; quite an inflation rate. Perhaps that is the way nurses should go. You may be a mere five-letter 'nurse' now, but you could expand into a nursor, then a nurseologist, and finally a nurseyopedologist. That's 17 letters! Of course if you do that the educationalists (16 letters) would insist on becoming educationopedopelists (21 letters). No matter how far we think we've come, the 'mine's bigger than yours' mentality still prevails, doesn't it?

Barbarella, meanwhile, attended an ENB research course this year at another former polytechnic with more than its fair share of inadequate tutors. Barbarella picked up a degree in the social sciences about 15 years ago before she came into nursing, but she readily admits that she has forgotten what she studied mostly because, like so many of us in those days, she went to polytechnic or university to have a bit of a laugh and to try to get laid. On the first day of the course, Barbie was told in hushed tones by some moron that this was a highly prestigious course, not to be trifled with. Indeed the standard was considered to be of degree level! Barbie and her colleagues were touched by the evangelical earnestness of the small man until he added, 'And you'll be pleased to know that nobody has ever failed!'

Too many nurse tutors want to sound like Bertrand Russell but look like Mickey Mouse.

Finally, my friend Rita Blood completed her Master's degree this year in health and social services. An experienced and intelligent woman, she was well supported by her trust and as part of that support she arranged to do her dissertation as a piece of active research reviewing the appropriateness and effectiveness of a large part of the service she worked in. It was a very good piece of work. However it contained useful information on clinical practice, problems assessment taken from notes and a breakdown of working practice on four wards. The university wrote to her and said this was not appropriate because they had no way of assessing the ethics of reflecting on real life. Rita informed them that they need not concern themselves because the work had been discussed with the trust ethics committee and the management group, and both had been encouraging. They said, and I quote: 'We've been running this course for four years but we've never had a piece of work that is based on real life before. Could you change it and re-submit it?' 'Is it not up to standard?' she asked. 'It is,' they said. 'In fact we are planning to offer you a distinction – it's just that, well, it's all a bit real isn't it?'

Nursing has changed to fit the universities; now they have to change to accommodate nursing. Have I mentioned that?

Yes, go on: do some academia. Take the courses that interest you. If you fancy a degree, do one that enlivens you. Do it in art or history or politics or philosophy or nursing. Do research if it warms your cockles. Teach – enthusiastically, passionately – but please don't pretend that thinking earnestly about something is an end in itself and please don't get all patronising. Personally I think all research and educational posts (and nursing journalism) should be integrated into nursing services, so that they are all rotated, and time away from practice for those who want it can be a process that enlivens and broadens clinical approaches. Let the support roles in nursing be used as a mechanism for retaining and supporting staff. Some argue that this would waste expertise. I disagree: most people fill these posts by design or coincidence, not pure talent. And if you develop skills thoughtfully they become transferable. We all know that too many relatively influential posts in academia are filled by 'nurses' who have no clinical experience. They are not in a position to integrate the concerns, framework or paradigm of practice with useful and considered curiosity.

Having said that I am aware that my mistrust and selective distaste for nursing academics is perhaps churlish and grating. It doesn't really bother me much but I just wanted to say that I am aware of it in case you thought I hadn't noticed. Nursing well is difficult, especially over a long period of time; thinking and theorising about it is, relative to sustaining good practice, dead easy.

There are of course some brilliant teachers around. You know who you are and more importantly so do your students. There is undoubtedly something very inspiring about great teachers. I'm not convinced by that funny advert where Tony Blair and other famous people who went to school say the name of an influential teacher. I can't remember any decent teachers at my school but I can recall some from polytechnic and university and, most importantly, from the school of nursing I trained in.

Our school of nursing was, in the main, ridiculous. Half of the staff wouldn't have known a patient if one had come up to them with a sandwich board declaring that he or she was, in fact, a patient. And they were crap teachers, bless them.

However there were two or three who taught really well. They managed to underpin our raw and powerful experiences with a knowledge base. They greeted our curiosity with a generosity and kindness which, on reflection, it did not always warrant. And most importantly they did not ever treat knowledge as an object.

Since that time I have worked with other teachers who seem blessed with patience, an understanding of nursing and outstanding communication skills. I rather envy that ability, but mostly I admire it. On listening to these people it seems that they are so good because they are interested in the students' experience and the well-being of the services they are involved with.

Similarly, for all my disdain of the plethora of would-be academics who have emerged in nursing, there are a handful of people who think or write or reflect or research nursing wonderfully. Even if you do not agree with them they arouse curiosity, introduce you to new ways of thinking about what you do and how you are involved in it, and teach as well.

Then there are the researchers. More often than not they are social scientists, quaintly determined to make sense of a confusing world. Somehow the demand for an evidence-based health service appears to have sneaked into government and collective consciousness. Personally, I think this is a misjudgement. Social science probably has its place – in my house, for example, its place is under the cooker – but it should certainly not be a premise for something as complex as health care. It can be a contributor if it likes, but that's all. If health care was Boyzone, for example, then evidence-based practice could be one of the little ones at the back who does harmonies but rarely takes the lead vocal. Then when Boyzone split up and the blonde one goes solo and one of the others goes into acting and turfs up on The Bill three months later, evidence-based practice might like to retire to a country home and count sheep, going on to conclude that there are a lot of sheep in the country, compared to the town. Despite everything that happened to evidence-based practice, through its years on the road, the women and the drugs, it always stayed true to itself. So when it came time to quit the big time it carried on counting stuff and making crass conclusions.

However, and this may come as a surprise to some of you, there is a new breed of researcher/academic in town: the new, vaguely philosophical, sort of post-structural post-modern type of nurse academic. They're great! You really ought to get one.

Papers by these people include 'Gestures of resistance: the nurse's body in contested space', which is basically about pushing and shoving in the dinner queue. And 'Post-modern feminist emancipatory research: is it an oxymoron?' Answer: yes, in fact it's probably about five oxymorons, which by lucky coincidence is the number of oxymorons you need to change a light bulb. My new favourite is 'Nursing's metaparadigm concepts: disimpacting the debates'. I understand the word 'nursing' but I'm lost after that. Is there such a word as 'disimpacting'? I don't think there is. I think the boffins over there are making up words.

You, however, are clearly on the brink of an academic career. Everything is going to be ordered and clever. You are going to operate, on our behalf, at the edges of common knowledge. You are going to push back those barriers. In this respect you academics are a bit like space warriors or polar explorers, all brave and purposeful, tackling issues like 'Nursing research and the philosophy of hermeneutics', and 'Typists' influence on transcription: aspects of feminist nursing epistemic rigour.'

You are brave bunnies and I want to help. I always want to help actually. I think it's a withdrawal-from-nursing thing. It doesn't matter if anyone wants any help; I just need to help. I like to help people on and off buses, for example, but being a busy boy I don't have time to ask them if they wish to board or depart the bus. I just rush on, grab the nearest person, often the conductor, and leap on to the pavement before the bus pulls off. I like helping.

So I thought I would offer up a glossary of helpful academic terms, just so you know what your new friends are talking about.

Ontology: thinking about being.

Epistemology: thinking about knowledge. Example of usage: the ontology of nursing: an epistemological crisis. Which, put another way, means nursing exists but we don't really know much about it.

Post modernism: the end of metaphysics.

Post structuralism: the end of metaphysics and that includes structuralism.

Structuralism: doesn't really matter because it's finished now. Gone. Dead. Nada. Kaput.

Postal orders: things that you buy from the Post Office when you want to pay for things that are advertised on television but you don't have a cheque book. A K-Tel record selector is a good example of something you may want to buy from the television.

Post feminism: the place successful middle-class women go to after they abandon feminism because they have no further use for it.

Post cards: little pictures of beaches and donkeys that you send to people to tell them that you are near beaches and donkeys.

There is however a real task ahead for those former nurses who now occupy the universities. The real question for them is whether or not they are prepared to take it on.

In other, more traditional areas of university life – like philosophy, grown-up sociology, politics, and history – thought reflects both the particulars of the field of concern and also the universal issues and implications that impact that area. People who think about nursing for a living seem strangely reluctant or currently ill-prepared to do that.

Good academics are aware of their history but not afraid or ashamed of it. Maybe they even play in the face of it. They act as a brake on the worst excesses of modern life as it trundles downhill ignoring the traffic lights. It is the job of academics to interpret the world around them, to criticise and proffer alternatives, to analyse cultural and social activity and thought, and to make sense of its obvious failings. Take the 1980s, for example. It wasn't a great decade. The creation of wealth became both the economic and the cultural premise. Every complex social activity was reduced to that simple expectation, and there was very little effective opposition to the excesses of privatisation, reduced public spending, and the Thompson Twins. The media rolled over and had its tummy tickled by Mrs Thatcher, the unions were either defeated (the miners) or spineless collaborators (the RCN) and the social fabric was revolutionised.

Arguably, the most consistent voice against the implications of what was going on all around us came from the universities. And they paid for it. They had little effect, and probably suffered as much as the hospitals, albeit in a different way. It was the job of the universities to commentate intelligently, critically and contextually on what was happening, to try to make some kind of philosophical sense of it. Most importantly, engaged academics would project the potential implications and stretch the cultural constructs that were dominant into social consequences and understanding. Irrelevant? No, an ongoing commentary of opposition may not be significant but it gives dissenters a voice. It does not have to be right, but its consistency and mere existence create a space for difference. If those commentators were wrong then so be it; they kept a space warm for others to come along and try to be less wrong. If nothing else, they functioned as a symbol of democracy and the place where possible alternatives could exist. They were committed to greater understanding. And at their best they led the field of ideas, political, social and philosophical. (Often they did this terribly – take the Adam Smith Institute, for example – but they did actually lead rather than just responding to the ground rules they were presented with and then meekly following, e.g. nursing and evidence-based practice.) Of course it was rarefied and often irrelevant but alternatives need to exist somewhere and ultimately that is what we pay thinkers for – to think. They have the time, the library cards and the relevant obsessions. The rest of us are too busy with real life.

Good academics pick at the stitches, and that is what nursing academics should be doing. That is what, eventually, they will have to do. The current problem of nursing academia is developmental. Half of them are social scientists who are so busy looking for wood that they keep bumping into trees. The other half have just discovered critical theory and are trying it on for size. There are maybe a handful of nursing academics who have transcended that nonsense and will think intelligently and contextually about what is happening to health care and to nursing and will write about it, critique it and give voice, intelligently, to the dissenters who may wish to re-humanise, re-invest or re-construct nursing and health care. Some more of them would be nice.

Sorry to sound old fashioned, but to be meaningful you are going to have to be political, with a small 'p'. Quite simply you cannot think about nursing without thinking about power relations. Regardless of what the UKCC or the RCN or the rest of the cast from Emergency Ward 10 think, what is happening politically in nursing is a disaster. Everyone is so busy chasing the minnows of nurse prescribing, nurse regulation, professionalisation, Primary Care Groups, etc, that they keep missing the big fish, the ones that require just a little vision. Like how to organise a modern National Health Service, how to finance it, how to develop effective investment in services and personnel, and how to sustain the staff and their skills. Nursing and its spokespeople really ought to stop humbly asking for permission to sit at the big table, get up off their arses and saw the table legs off.

In the main, academics are undeveloped in nursing. That will probably change; your generation will maybe change it. I hope so.

The politicians however are just pathetic and because most of them are not elected (does that happen anywhere else?) you can't vote them out. By and large they are self-serving, visionless bureaucrats who are so desperate to impress the Civil Service and the Press that they don't dare surprise themselves with anything that might resemble a decent idea. On the plus side, however, I understand that a lot of them have lovely singing voices.

If there is hope anywhere it is in the probability that political and intellectual trends tend to move in something like circles and the simplistic nonsense that lingers from the 1980s is already beginning to seem dated, inflexible and useless. There is an atmosphere of disaffection illustrated by the number of people leaving nursing and the dissatisfaction of many of those who stay. And some, more adventurous thinkers are working and working well.

To what extent any of this actually affects the working experience of nurses remains to be seen. But perhaps that is the challenge: to devise pressure, criticism and ideas that describe in a meaningful way the circumstances and difficulties that nurses have.

However there remain some outstanding pieces of pertinent and potentially revolutionary research to admire. Take for example the startling results of a study by US researchers. Apparently, and I hope you are sitting down for this, nurses who get migraines are significantly less productive when they have a headache than nurses without headaches. Furthermore, nurses who get migraines also have a reduced quality of life compared with nurses who don't get migraines.

These stunning revelations were gathered after researchers sampled a massive 10 000 nurses. They concluded that nasty headaches really do hurt. They could have saved a lot of stamps if someone had just had the far-sightedness to slap them hard round the back of the head and ask them if they felt as productive as they had done pre-slap. I gather this is called participatory observation.

Further examples of the stunning investigation into the obvious include: Hopping: exactly how many feet do you need for that? The blindfolded nurse in the community; should she really be driving?

And, Are nurses who wear belts more effective than nurses who wear braces?

One suspects that clinical trials were involved in drawing up the final conclusion about headaches and productivity. However the idea of making nurses with migraines work under clinically controlled conditions is too inhumane even for the Americans, so they had to use animals.

Basically they got some laboratory rats to dress up as nurses, induced in them migraine headaches and compared them to ordinary headacheless nurses. Of course, the normal headacheless nurses had a far better sense of the routine of the ward and could also reach things a little more easily than the rats, so they instantly appeared far more productive. However the looseness of this clinical trial was such that the researchers were concerned about the validity of their results, so they did the whole thing again, replacing the headacheless nurses with more rats, this time without headaches.

Things went well at first. The difference in productivity was marked. The rats who were not in pain wandered around sniffing the floor, made the occasional bed and hung around outside the toilets, whilst the rats with headaches lay on the floor asking for the lights to be dimmed and having cold towels draped across their temples. But then things began to go wrong.

All the rats were borrowed from the science lab and they had previously experienced many different types of experiment. Some of the 'let's see if rats that smoke 40 a day are less able to cycle up a hill than non-smoking rats' contingent began to develop little coughs and insisted on the researchers providing a smoking room. The researchers were worried. Did this point to the possibility that rats with coughs were less productive on the ward than rats that didn't cough? Then some of the rats who had been part of an experiment involving chemical weapons began to turn green and bits of rat fell off. Others who had been given typhoid just upped and died before the end of the shift, whilst others who had been involved in testing the effects of excessive alcohol intake just pissed off down the pub.

The researchers were in a quandary. How were they to know, absolutely, without question and irrefutably, that nurses with nasty headaches were less able to run around like blue-arsed flies than nurses without? So they guessed, and I think you'll agree they probably got it right. Just to check it out they wrote to 10,000 people and asked them about headaches. But in truth they had to do that anyway because the cost of 10,000 stamps was part of the original research proposal and you've got to use up all the money or you look like amateurs.

The Politicians and the Managers

◆ ◆ ◆ ◆ ◆ ◆ ◆

Politicians in nursing are an ever-expanding group, usually terribly dressed and occasionally well meaning. If you are anything like me you won't come across this group of people much in practice. If you'd asked me who the chief nurse was, or the general secretary of the RCN, or anything like that whilst I was nursing I would not have had a clue. Nor would I have hung about to hear you tell me because I would have assumed that you were very dull.

Of course, if you'd asked me some questions about pop music, or sport, or something a little more personal like what's my favourite colour I'd have hung about for ages, probably asking you about your hobbies and your favourite shirt. Oh yes, we'd have got on very nicely, maybe going for a drink after work. But nursing politicians, no.

However, in recent times it has come to my attention that there are all sorts of austere and slightly posh people out there trying to do their best to enhance their careers and, even more importantly, maintain the status quo. Not the Status Quo obviously. I would not suggest for one moment that there are anxious and overworked former nurses in varying positions of power using their energies and skills to force a comeback from the denim-clad rockers best known perhaps for 'Rocking All Over the World'. That would be silly. No, these people work pretty hard, pretending to change things – which pretty much means that things stay the same. But fair's fair, they all have their own teeth.

Nursing has long held a massive inferiority complex when it looks at medicine. I don't quite know why. It may have something to do with 'A' levels or the fact that doctors don't have to wear stupid hats. More likely, it's something to do with gender. There has also long been a cultural tendency for nurses to nurse doctors (metaphorically of course; clearly nurses don't hand out bed baths or drugs to doctors. That would be foolish and a waste of sponge). You facilitate, because it is in the nature of nursing. The word nursing is derived from the same root as 'to nourish' and you have long nourished doctors. Which is ever so nice of you.

It seems to me that the whole 'let's be more like doctors' thing is a bit of red herring, but I'm sure it's all being done for the best. Except nothing really changes. The patients still need nursing, the nurses still deserve better money. Still on the bright side ... No, I can't think of anything at the moment; I'll get back to you about the bright side.

The main problem nursing has with people who politic is the sort of role models they choose. Too often top nurses dress like Edwina Curry, talk like Margaret Thatcher and think like La La the Teletubby. Nursing is crying out for someone to sweep into a packed conference hall like Katherine Hepburn, spitting blood, mocking the conservatism that is attached to the profession, doing great things and scaring people. Who on Earth is ever going to be afraid of the nursing politicians we have? It's all well and good saying 'Yes, but they have to play the game', but what does that really mean? Trying so hard to fit in, using the same language, the same vision as the BMA or the Civil Service or any of the crusty organisations that actually marginalised nursing in the first place? Why is it that all these bureaucrats just seem to roll over and die every time something important happens, like staged pay awards and the internal market?

Of course we cannot confine our idle chatter to the large handful of political figures in nursing. We need to extend the use of our metaphorical water pistols to those other merchants of power in nursing: the managers. And I don't mean ward managers or team leaders here. They tend to be referred to as managers only when they are being asked to make budget savings.

A lot of us have said some pretty horrid things about managers in the past and it's worth noting that not one of us regrets a single barbed comment. It's constantly fascinating that rabidly reactionary commentators openly discuss the route to management positions and try to encourage perfectly sensible nurses to do MBAs.

Imagine, as I'm sure you can, that we are all living in an episode of The Waltons. Imagine also that we are not going to spend the next month arguing about who gets to be John Boy or Jim Bob or Billy Ray or Biffy Boo or whoever they all were. Just that we all lived on Walton Mountain and every day we tried to do good in the face of temptation and poverty and that, in the main, we succeeded. And despite the fact that we had to wear dungarees all the bloody time we were quite happy. Imagine, if you like, that on the other side of Walton Mountain was Little House on the Prairie. Sometimes, on our day off, we would all go over there to play with those smashing children in their delightful smocks. Now imagine that, as we were all going to church one Sunday to thank the good Lord for Walton Mountain, our endless supply of bibs and denim and those nice prairie kids, Satan was outside the church trying to get us to apply to do an MBA, with his prince of darkness promises of endless paper clips and our own voice mail. That is how the drive to encourage nurses to become managers looks to me.

Now before you say, 'Oi, dopey boy, are you suggesting that nurses should not take up positions of responsibility, nor develop their careers according to their interests, nor move on naturally when they feel it is appropriate without them standing accused of being the devil's spawn?' I would say, 'No, and don't call me dopey boy, carrot breath!' We all know that most nurses go into management because they believe that they can save services, because they want to stop or at least slow the dismantling of their wards, and of course because they may well want to see what it's like to live on a reasonably decent wage for the first time in their lives. Under the circumstances they may have saved hospitals, services and jobs through their efforts but at what cost?

The problem with going into management positions is one of collaboration. It may appear absolutely necessary, it may be the only way open and I would not criticise any individual for doing it, but within the context of nursing it is a cultural development that has had some pretty dire consequences. On the up side, and I'm sure the RCN are thrilled with this, it raises expectations for nurses, gives the impression of more able nurses (actually I'm unconvinced by this) and creates at least the illusion of power. On the down side, all it means is that during a period of history which has seen a freezing of pay and a restraint on conditions for nurses, a reduction of gross product investment in the NHS, an increase in waiting lists, a reduction in real terms of beds and an increase in privatisation (which has undermined the principle of the best available care for all, regardless of ability to pay) and the compounding trend of rises in prescription costs, etc, a structure has been created in which nurses as managers, often with the best will in the world, have done the dirty work. In short, with purchasers and providers and contract managers and budget management at ward and service level, and service capping and all the other modern market-led inventions, it means that nurses are screwing nurses, and I don't mean that in a good way. For all the good done by considerate, enthusiastic and thoughtful individuals in their efforts to save the health service, they have mediated the most destructive period in the history of nursing. And that destruction could not have happened without them. When that nice Mrs Thatcher and all those blubbery boys in the 1980s announced the shape of things to come, if everyone had just said, 'Go right ahead love, but I'm not going to help,' then they would have been stuffed. It's not as if Mrs T had a stockpile of equipped and knowledgeable managers hanging around in her kitchen, ready to take over the hospitals at a moment's notice. She relied absolutely on the collaboration of willing and easily led would-be managers.

I know, I know, I know; nothing is that simple. We had no way of knowing. A consciousness of opposition did not really exist at that time and anyway we all knew that things had to change. Besides, idealising about unity and resistance is naïve and romantic. I almost agree, but the point remains: it was ambitious wanna-please managers who administered the policies which dismantled services and ultimately disempowered nurses and patients alike. Do you believe for a moment that modernity has blessed you with professional autonomy now because you can sign a script for paracetamol and get to make up the numbers on primary care groups? Half the nurses you have left behind on the wards don't feel empowered enough to actually do any bloody nursing any more. Still that's progress for you.

There is no doubting, of course, that you managers are very important. Lord knows what we would do with the NHS budget if we didn't have you lot to give it to in the form of stupid salaries (managing is easier than nursing, ergo managers should not get paid three or four times more than nurses ... Discuss). And of course in bonus payments ...

Barbarella used to run a rehabilitation ward for the older person. One day her manager visited the thriving ward, wandered around a bit and finally gathered the staff together. She thanked them for their fine efforts in accelerating the turn-around time of patients which meant that they had produced a large increase in admissions and discharges, by working effectively with social services and follow-up services. She said that she was particularly pleased because their good work had resulted in a generous performance-related pay bonus for her. She had no sense of how this would be experienced by the staff, other than imagining that they should be selflessly pleased for her and that their main motivation had been her financial well-being. And they wonder about morale?

Perhaps bonus payments are the way forward for nurses. The idea of a bonus payment, as you probably know, is that if you do the job you are paid to do without messing it up you get paid extra. Nurses should get bonus payments. If you run a ward, say for a shift, and during that shift the ward does not accidentally turn into a boating lake in Southern France or just get up and wander off without telling the patients or the staff, then you should get a bonus of sorts. It's unlikely but it may be a way forward for pay negotiators.

However, managers are far more important than anyone else. In fact the only people more important than managers are other managers. There are few things in life as entertaining as watching a bunch of macho managers telling each other how busy they are.

A good friend, who has to do some managing but chooses to do it in the style of Emma Peel, was recently at some meeting that was full of other managers – service managers, district managers, nurse managers, contract managers; hundreds of the bastards. It was decided that all of these managers had so much managing to do that they should go on an awayday; a managers' awayday. This meeting took place in early August, and they all reached for their diaries.

The buildings manager said that she was going to have trouble finding a window before late September (sub text: I'm busy, don't make me redundant, buildings don't just manage themselves you know). The nurse manager, a former goalkeeper with Leyton Orient, said that he had no space until November (sub text: I'm twice as important as the woman in charge of buildings). The contract manager announced that she was choc-a-block right through until the following February (sub text: I am so important I've already got my next year's diary from the stationery office). The buildings manager, who was feeling a bit insecure and very pissed off with stationery for not giving her a diary for next year and, more importantly, not telling her that the contract manager had one and it was one of those nice blue ones as well, countered: 'Well I need it to be before October because after then things really get mad for me. The buildings need a lot of managing between October and the following May.'

The district manager, who didn't really get what his job was but liked the office and had never had his own secretary before, sighed, 'It's going to be very difficult for me to make a space before next June.'

Finally my friend Emma Peel said, 'What about next Tuesday?' and everyone flicked through their diaries.

The buildings manager said, 'Oh, I can't do that.'

'Why not?'

'It's too short notice. There will be no time for memos to everyone.'

'Do we need memos? After all everyone is here ...'

'Do we need memos?' blustered the buildings manager, 'What are you, some kind of anarchist? Of course we need memos. The health service without memos is like a tree without leaves. Why, do you not remember the great memo of '95 telling staff not to wear their underpants outside their trousers? It was brilliant in its irrelevance. And the one about health promotion and smoking.'

'Didn't someone set fire to that?'

At this point a mysterious manager who attended these meetings all the time but nobody knew what he managed, pulled out an electronic organiser.

'Wow, what's that?'

'Oh this,' he said nonchalantly, 'This is just my diary.'

'It's great,' said the contract manager. 'It's so shiny. Does it run on batteries?'

'Yes.'

'I love things that run on batteries,' said the nursing manager.

'It has many functions.'

'I LOVE things that have many functions,' said the nursing manager.

'It tells the time, has three computer games, it plays 'Won't You Come Home Bill Bailey' at the end of the working day and it tells me what day it is in Bangkok.'

'I LOVE things that have many functions,' repeated the nursing manager.

Emma Peel reports that very few decisions were made that day, beyond the fact that all the managers made requests for electronic organisers. The mysterious man who managed they-knew-not-what, took on the mantle of hero. He later revealed to the enthralled administrators that he had a bleep, a pager and a mobile phone, and the buildings manager had an orgasm.

Probably the most irritating thing about managers, however, is unfortunately implicit in their job. They get to tell you what you can and can't do with your service. If you need extra staff, it is their job to tell you that you can't have them. If you don't feel you can, under the circumstances, operate the service safely or in accordance with its stated aims, they persuade you (or try to) to carry on regardless. They are the ones who force down-grading of open posts and stop G grades working weekends regardless of service needs. And they are the ones who tell you about pointless, expensive and ill-considered organisational changes just when you are getting used to the last lot of pointless, expensive and ill-considered organisational changes. And have you noticed that every time there is an organisational change it seems to coincide with the loss of clinical time and a new management post that is given to someone who was previously in a management post but who actually, they realised, didn't have anything to do? I suspect that the mysterious manager at Emma Peel's meeting didn't actually manage anything. He was just a spare that they keep hanging around on a 40K retainer waiting for the next reshuffle.

At the same time, this is probably the place where the really hard bit of managing happens and if you are going to manage you may find it the no-win situation.

Daniel currently works as a service manager overseeing three wards with about 47 staff. By coincidence, recently about six of them fell pregnant. Daniel asked no questions concerning last year's Christmas party. Instead he set about trying to figure out how all of these valued members of staff could best be supported in a flexible way if and when they returned to work after giving birth.

He was approached by one pregnant member of staff and told that in future she would only be available to work Monday to Thursday, 9 to 3, with no possibility of anything else. Under the circumstances, this seemed a perfectly legitimate request, though probably impossible to sanction without some thought. So Daniel said that he could not promise anything but he would hate to lose her so he would see what he could do.

She told her colleagues, with the bravado that often haunts a staff room, that she had demanded and received assurances that she could work the hours she wanted. And so Daniel was met with similar demands from the others on the basis that if he was going to do that for her he must do the same for them. As the domino effect kicked in, and before Daniel had had the opportunity to talk properly to anyone, the rest of the un-pregnant staff were complaining that this constituted discrimination and that they were not prepared to have their shift patterns and off-duty dominated by the demands of the pregnant ones. At no point did the staff talk to each other about this; that was the manager's responsibility. It became an area in which to act out all the hostility and resentment that the hospital managers had generated amongst the staff over the previous three years.

Daniel was charged with sorting it out. And so he did the only thing he could: he went to the staff, explained the problem and asked them for their ideas. For this he stood accused of trying to drive a wedge between the staff, which was perhaps a consequence of doing what he did. In the end he did what good managers have to do – set limits and explain them clearly. Things settled down apparently and three of the pregnant women did not return to work. However they had privately made it clear that they had never intended to do so.

I'll come back to trying to be nice to the managers again in a minute. It feels a bit like swimming underwater: I can only do it for so long before my lungs ache.

One of the funniest types of manager or administrator lives in the room that used to be called the personnel office but is now known only as 'human resources'. These people are responsible for advertising and filling new posts, arranging induction and generally resourcing anything that requires humans. They have been known to place adverts for jobs so slowly that the closing dates for applications are actually a week before the advert is published. They arrange induction into the trust for people who have been working in their service for three years. On one occasion someone I know was sent on induction three days before he left for another job. If you apply for a job and are told 'If you have not heard within three weeks then please assume that you are on this occasion not successful,' don't believe it. I was told this once, did not hear anything for four weeks and forgot about it. I got a phone call six weeks after the closing date asking me why I was not at the interview they had arranged for me. I said I had not been informed of an interview and they sighed and said that happened a lot. Apparently the human resources department was very busy on an audit of their services; they may have forgotten to write. I got a letter offering me the interview I had missed, ten days after I wasn't there.

Deep breath.

Of course, you the manager may find yourself facing unreasonable requests that are not always easily dealt with. My friend who manages like Emma Peel, for example, received a request from a music therapist to have her contract extended to full time from a part-time post so that she could be supported in doing extra clinical work and paid for studying a Masters degree in 'translating music psychoanalytically for a bit of a laugh'. She was told no. The music therapist tried to put together a petition to save the music therapist. If people signed it, it was to make her go away and take her stupid tuba with her. Emma Peel explained that the service could not afford, nor indeed felt the need, to extend her input.

The music therapist wrote to her MP. The MP wrote to Emma Peel. Emma Peel shrugged. The music therapist staged a one-woman demonstration by abseiling down the side of the Post Office with a cello strapped to her back. Emma Peel again said no. Finally the music therapist went to the consultant on the ward and lay at his feet, wailed and kicked her tap shoes against the floor. The consultant admitted her.

Managing issues such as short course funding will be a nightmare. There is no doubt that many managers do this really badly, often by using up the whole budget on their own needs – needs that are met by management consultancy groups who run two-day workshops in 'the use of special manager words in meetings with staff' (words like download, re-sizing, floating investment and invest-rotational funding ... no, I don't know either).

However Emma Peel reports employing a support worker for a community mental health team, who threatened to resign after six weeks unless the whole of his psychotherapy training was paid for. When asked how a psychotherapy training would help him do his job, he replied, 'I'd be able to provide psychotherapy.'

'But that's not what the patients need from a support worker, that is not what we employed you for.'

'But that's what I'd like to do.'

'Yes, yes, but that's not what the patients need and that is not what we funded the post for.'

'But it's what I want to do.'

'I understand that but oddly enough the services were not designed to meet your needs.'

'But it's important that you meet the needs of the staff.'

'Indeed it is, but I think you'll agree there are limits. In fact we call them boundaries. For example, if the registrar wanted to become a paratrooper, would it be my responsibility to buy him a plane so he could practice?'

'You're being silly now.'

'You're not getting the bloody money.'

'I'll leave.'

'OK.'

'It'll be your fault.'

'OK.'

'The patients love me. You are depriving them of consistency of care.'

'How much trouble do you actually have taking responsibility for yourself?'

'I don't know. I haven't done my psychotherapy training yet.'

There is no doubt that some of the work managers have to do is very difficult. However, there is little doubt that extensive clinical experience is the best tool available to managers, particularly when they are near the coal face, so to speak. Whilst ideologically there are problems with going into management – namely the role they play in sustaining the system they find themselves involved with on a day-to-day level, most nurses would rather be managed by someone who knows the experience, the language and the concerns of practice than by someone who did an MBA, or used to run a chain of pet shops or who trained in a supermarket.

Managers become more absurd the further away they are from practice. There are increasing numbers of managers associated to health trusts who reflect the corporate nature of modern NHS organisation.

My favourite group of managers are the newest ones. They are the people who run the communications office of the modern health trusts. You'd think that the communications manager would be in charge of memos and the internal telephone links, but that's the memo and telephone manager. The communications manager is in charge of PR. In this corporate world, trusts are concerned with public image and so they have their own spin doctors. These people have to write policies on how to deal with the media. So, for example, if you write a paper about an aspect of your practice you have to inform them and have it cleared. If you write a column for Nursing Times about something to do with your profession, you have to clear it with them. If you are phoned up as a clinician and asked your opinion about something in the news, you have to say, 'I'm sorry I have to get clearance from my communications office before I can talk to you.'

This defensiveness is born of fear. Perhaps too many managers read the tabloids and imagine that if they speak to a journalist they are going to be 'quoted out of context' or be airbrushed into a photograph of Saddam Hussein and portrayed as his sexual plaything. A shade paranoid I fear, but there you go.

It's a strange thought that as nursing diversifies in its specialisms, methods, opinions and cultures, any variation in its voice is quietened by the corporate way of modern health organisation. As a consequence your opinions, input and insight into any of the issues that surround your work, your profession, or the policies that regulate you are not allowed. What is allowed is the passive bleating of media officers, PR people and professional organisations. It amounts to a none-too-subtle way of disqualifying the nurses' voice. This is happening at the same time that professional organisations and unions are supposedly encouraging the nurses' voice – so long as the voice says what it is told to say, and doesn't ask questions. Personally I choose naïveté. If you have something to say, best say it; better out than in. If it makes you nervous, tell the journalists not to use your name, or better still invent a name. I think it would be good if all nurses who talked to the media got together first and came up with one name, something like Jules Bratpacker, and then every time a nurse was quoted as saying something about the closure of services or under-staffing, or overtime shenanigans, or policy errors or whatever, one name would rise above the crowd and denounce the unfairness and it would be the name of Jules Bratpacker. Nobody would ever see Jules; nobody would know if Jules was a he or a she. All they would know is that Jules spoke out for the downtrodden. Jules was an urban guerrilla, a space warrior, a hero of the people. And Jules would be a mystery, they-seek-him-here-they-seek-her-there kind of voice.

Back to the politicians, the ones who politic essentially with the UKCC, the RCN, UNISON and all those other organisations committed to the well-being of nursing. How do you get to work for them then?

I'm not sure if it's true but as I understand it the RCN, and the UKCC, etc, tend to hoover up those of you who are called 'the bright sparks'. That is what I am told. I'll be honest: I have no way of knowing. I never met anyone who worked for any of those organisations when I was in practice, and when I stumbled across what they said about my particular area, I, like most of the people I worked with, thought they were funny. But all that really means is that I was never a bright spark and nor were my friends. The bright sparks who politicked broadly on our behalf had better things to do than talk to us.

Now that I'm not in practice I get more time to read and listen to what these people say, and I can honestly tell you with my hand on my heart that my friends and I were right: they are quite funny. They remind me of a bit in a Bruce Lee film called Enter the Dragon. Yes, I know that most of you are either too sophisticated, too young or too gentle to watch Bruce Lee films, but tough; I'm being post modern. Bruce plays a Shaolin monk who is sent off to fight bad people. However, before he goes we find him in the Shaolin temple giving a lesson to a funny looking boy with a silly haircut. After a bit of teaching, he realises that the boy is not really paying attention;

he doesn't seem to be getting what Bruce is telling him. So Bruce slaps the boy on the haircut (this was 1973; Shaolin monks did that sort of thing then), points to the sky and asks, 'What do you see?' The boy says, 'Er, the moon?' And Bruce says something like, 'Don't look at the moon or you will miss all the heavenly glory.' I was 13; what can I say? Anyway that whole looking-at-the-moon-and-missing-all-the-sky thing, that's what I think the little politicians do. They miss the point. I'm sure they are all very nice but they seem to be grinding themselves into a kind of bureaucratic mincemeat.

What is the alternative? Well I think that to start with the RCN UNISON and the UKCC should all be turned into musical bureaucracies. Everything they do, every meeting they have, every silly self-indulgent little pronouncement they make should be in the form of a song. Give the Code of Conduct to Andrew Lloyd Webber; he's worked with worse and the crowds have flocked in. Loosen the little buggers up a bit. Who would not respect the RCN more if their General Secretary sang 'Just a Spoonful of Sugar Makes the Medicine Go Down' instead of giving another pointless speech at next year's congress? And UNISON: I don't know why, but when I think UNISON I think Slade singing 'Cum on Feel the Noize' but they could update (it's about time), maybe with a bit of Celine Dion or Oasis, who I personally think are Slade reborn. Even as you go in the door to any of the above organisations, you would be met with a showtime tune and the man on the door doing a Dick Van Dyke cockney accent whilst singing 'Chim-chimeney'. It wouldn't make them any more effective but it would make them more interesting.

Deep breath.

OK everyone's doing their best and nobody is probably to blame for anything. Everything is beyond everyone's control, we are all trying to make it better and it's best if we pull in the same direction. We should trust in our leaders, the politicians, because they know what's best and they are well informed and capable of the appropriate analysis of what is possible at any given time. The fact that it seems that they are all in competition with each other for members, subscriptions, the last word, the best jobs, the right way, etc, can't be helped. It will all be all right; it will come out in the wash; a bird in the hand is worth two in the bush. Let's just be patient. Wait a while. It'll be OK in a minute.

We'll just wait here.

Not long now.

A pay rise is just round the corner, and better conditions, less stress, some new shoes, eternal happiness. Former nurses are going to flock back, and new nurses, thousands of them, longing to nurse, dreaming of the day they will get their own whistle. It's just around the corner.

Won't be long.

Any day now.

Here it comes. The wheels of change are on the bus of opportunity and it's towing our ship which is coming in, and our ship is full of bicycles of love and ponies, free and happy ponies, ponies who are grateful to you, with baby ponies who would not be here if it wasn't for you, baby ponies on our ship which is coming in who want to say a great big thank you to you, and to give you bicycles of love or seats on the bus of opportunity. And it's all thanks to the stirring work of our representatives. They are not just frightened jobsworths; I was wrong all the time. They did know best; they were just biding their time until the right moment. Here comes the right moment.

In a minute.

Here it comes.

Any generation now.